# LAYMAN'S LIBRARY OF CHRISTIAN DOCTRINE

## What Is Christian Doctrine?

### JOHN P. NEWPORT

**BROADMAN PRESS**
Nashville, Tennessee

*To*

*Martha Newport Gay*

*Kim Cooper Newport*

*Mary Dell Harrington Newport*

Beloved daughter and daughters-in-law

significant laypersons in my life

© Copyright 1984 ● Broadman Press

All rights reserved

4216-31

ISBN: 0-8054-1631-5

Dewey Decimal Classification: 230

Subject Heading: THEOLOGY

Library of Congress Catalog Card Number: 83-71266

Printed in the United States of America

**Library of Congress Cataloging in Publication Data**

Newport, John P., 1917-
  What is Christian doctrine?

  Bibliography: p.
  Includes index.
  1. Theology, Doctrinal.   I. Title.
BT75.2.N49   1984      230'.01        83-71266
ISBN 0-8054-1631-5

# Contents

# Foreword

The *Layman's Library of Christian Doctrine* in sixteen volumes covers the major doctrines of the Christian faith.

To meet the needs of the lay reader, the *Library* is written in a popular style. Headings are used in each volume to help the reader understand which part of the doctrine is being dealt with. Technical terms, if necessary to the discussion, will be clearly defined.

The need for this series is evident. Christians need to have a theology of their own, not one handed to them by someone else. The *Library* is written to help readers evaluate and form their own beliefs based on the Bible and on clear and persuasive statements of historic Christian positions. The aim of the series is to help laypeople hammer out their own personal theology.

The books range in size from 140 pages to 168 pages. Each volume deals with a major part of Christian doctrine. Although some overlap is unavoidable, each volume will stand on its own. A set of the sixteen-volume series will give a person a complete look at the major doctrines of the Christian church.

Each volume is personalized by its author. The author will show the vitality of Christian doctrines and their meaning for everyday life. Strong and fresh illustrations will hold the interest of the reader. At times the personal faith of the authors will be seen in illustrations from their own Christian pilgrimage.

Not all laypeople are aware they are theologians. Many may believe they know nothing of theology. However, every person believes something. This series helps the layperson to understand what he believes and to be able to be "prepared to make a defense to anyone who calls him to account for the hope that is in him" (1 Pet. 3:15).

# 1
# Every Person Believes Something

## All Persons Have a Belief System

Do you realize that there are no atheists? Of course, there are some people who do not believe in and follow the God revealed in the Hebrew prophets and Jesus Christ. But there are no atheists. Each person has a supreme source of meaning (conscious or unconscious) for his or her day-by-day decisions and life purposes.

A part of being human is to have some sort of belief system. Everyone has a theology, a world view, or a particular way of looking at the world. We may be largely unaware of the beliefs which are at the heart of our thinking and acting, but we all believe something.

The most important question that can be asked about a person is, What is the belief system that guides your moral decisions and the use of your time and money and that colors your attitudes? The answer to this question will shape the quality and influence of your life.

## Your Belief System Is Based on a Key Idea or "God"

There are no practical or psychological atheists. Deep in the structure of your personality is an absolute or final value, a faith principle, or your god. A crisis will reveal the key category of your belief system.

Joshua told the assembled people of Israel, "Choose this day whom you will serve" (Josh. 24:15). The early Christians also realized that you either worship the God of Jesus Christ or some other god. A man once told me, "There ain't a thing in life but eating and drinking." He worshiped the god of gluttony or immediate physical satisfaction.

Historically, most Americans have said they were followers of the God of Jesus Christ. Some polls show 90 percent of the American people say they believe in God. However, day-by-day living shows materialism dominates many lives.The proper question is, What (Who) is your God?

## The Christian Has a Distinctive World View
## or Belief System

The early Christians were grasped by a unique view of history and life. They accepted the teaching that the personal, Creator God voluntarily revealed himself in mighty deeds and words through particular events and people. For them, God entered history in divine acts and raised up persons to interpret the significance of these acts. In the Old Testament, Christians see the beginning of God's redemptive revelation of himself to humanity. The continuation and fulfillment of God's saving revelation is in the New Testament.

In the Old Testament, Christians see God working for justice and redemptive love in history. In the New Testament, God is further pictured as the God of forthgoing love who shares in the grief and need of his creatures. When a person embraces Christ as Savior and Lord, he also embraces a new world view or belief system, reflecting the character and purpose of God.

The churches in Germany were relatively strong in the 1930s. Could the Christians be led to support the semipagan, nationalistic Nazi movement? The Nazis applied social, political, and economic pressure. Some professing Christians succumbed and either went along with the Nazis or failed to protest. Other Christians took a strong stand against the Nazis. One dramatic protest was that of Martin Niemöller. A former submarine commander in the German navy, he had become a prominent Protestant pastor. One Sunday he preached on the subject, "God Alone Is My *Fuehrer*" (leader). The Nazi Storm Troopers were present in his church that Sunday to take Niemöller to prison.

In twentieth-century America, few Christians are forced in such a dramatic way to defend or identify their faith. But we must remember that the Christian faith is distinctive. We need to clearly define its content and implications in each generation.

## Christian Doctrine Is the Systematic Development
## of the Revealed Christian World View

We begin our study of Christian doctrine with the understanding that in the many stories and teachings of the Bible one can find the ingredients for a distinctive world view. But the collection of the apostles' writings found in the New Testament, for example, is not systematically organized. Christian theology seeks to draw out from the Bible's testimony of what God has done and to teach a systematic belief system. Christian doctrine is a thought-out order and framework which can help us understand better and share more effectively the Christian faith.

As we shall see, Christian doctrine must be restated in each age since it is necessarily formulated in the thought forms of a particular time. Because of this fact, many Protestant groups call their Christian doctrinal statements "confessions of faith." Since the gospel is intended for all persons, Christian doctrine should be written so that it is understandable by laymen as well as by specialists.

In Matthew's Gospel (16:15-16), we are told that Jesus asked his disciples, "Who do you say that I am?" Peter answered this question by stating that "You are the Christ, the Son of the living God." This is one of the first Christian theological confessions or doctrinal statements.

In each generation and in each broad geographical or cultural area, it has been important to state the basic Christian teachings in clear language and thought forms. Attempts to formulate Christian doctrine in each generation involve the risk of changing or watering down the Christian gospel. The responsibility of the theologian is to preserve the unchanging content of the biblical revelation and yet apply it creatively to each generation.

In summary, Christian doctrine seeks to give a clear and organized statement of the teachings of the Christian faith based primarily on the Bible. It further seeks to place this statement in the context of culture. In order to relate to culture, Christian doctrine should be worded in contemporary and understandable language and should be related to the living issues of life.

### Bibliography

Keeley, Robin, ed. *Eerdmans' Handbook to Christian Belief.* Grand Rapids, MI: Wm. B. Eerdmans, 1982.
Smart, James D. *What a Man Can Believe.* Philadelphia: Westminster Press, 1953.
Wells, William W. *Welcome to the Family: An Introduction to Evangelical Christianity.* Downers Grove, IL: InterVarsity Press, 1979.

# 2
# The Crucial Importance of Christian Doctrine

In today's world, a person must have a unifying and clear-cut world view if he or she is to live successfully and positively. There are endless things to do, endless places to go, and unnumbered possible vocations. We need a world view or doctrinal system to rank possible activities and set priorities. Moral decisions, time utilization, financial management, family life—all these are affected. In a broader sense, we need to unify our thoughts and life, define the good life, guide thought and action, and find hope and meaning in life. The Christian conviction is that Christian doctrine can furnish this needed world view.

It should be helpful to list in more specific detail some of the reasons for the crucial importance of Christian doctrine.

## Christian Doctrine Helps Us Share the Christian Gospel

The first impulse of a Christian is to get the Christian message out to as many people as possible. But we must remember that it is important to first get the Christian message straight. Christian doctrine helps us understand, define, and explain Christianity to others.

## Christian Doctrine Shapes or Determines Our Actions

Of course, knowledge can never be a substitute for responsible action. But beliefs have a great deal to do with action and attitude. On a trip to the People's Republic of China, I saw the programs and definite actions which have resulted from the Communist doctrine which has been taught for over thirty years. In the long run, beliefs do help determine actions.

The dominant beliefs of a society put a stamp on its approach to life. I saw the result of the impact of belief systems in visits to Egypt (Islamic belief system) and Thailand (Buddhist belief system). Legal systems are even determined by religious values in Islamic countries such as Iran.

Christian doctrine teaches that God is the God of righteousness and justice. This means that those embracing Christian doctrine will realize that what is right and just on earth is important and worth contending for.

Christian doctrine also states that God is the God of caring love as revealed in Jesus Christ. This means that Christians will seek to live lives of loving concern for those in need and not just seek a mystical spiritual state of ecstasy for themselves, as do some Hindu religious groups. A nation that is dominated by atheism or secularism does not see human beings as made in God's image and thus of infinite worth. With the loss of this biblical conviction about human nature, there will be a tendency to look at people as animals or machines. And if we are mere machines, it is meaningless to speak of good and evil and moral responsibility. A person tends to act out what he believes. In contrast, Christian doctrine teaches that a Christian should be a universal citizen and not be bound by cultural, regional, class, or racial captivity. He should serve all people who hurt throughout the world because they are of infinite worth.

A crucial problem in the Christian community is the difference between the Christian world view or doctrine which we nominally confess and the world view which is reflected in our practical living. This problem was even present in the early Christian church. While in Joppa (modern Jaffa in Israel), we were shown a mosque built on the traditional site where Peter had his vision that there was no unclean thing (Acts 10:9-19). In this vision, Peter was taught by God that a Christian should not be a respecter of persons and the gospel of grace must be preached to all people (Acts 10:17-48). Immediately after the vision, Peter had visitors from the household of Cornelius, the Gentile centurion, requesting that Peter come to Caesarea to preach to this ceremonially unclean group. Peter agreed to go to Caesarea and preach to the Gentiles.

And yet Galatians 2:11-14 tells the very human and tragic story of Peter lapsing back into his old world view in the presence of a group of conservative Jewish Christians in Antioch. Paul had to remind Peter that it was essential to the gospel of grace to include all people who believe.

Those who experienced firsthand the life, death, and resurrection of Christ had problems in changing personal world views. That should remind twentieth-century Christians of the difficulty and yet the urgency of making Christian doctrine real and practical in our lives. This need points up the importance of dynamic Bible study, doctrinal study, regular worship, and the empowerment of the Holy Spirit.

## Christian Doctrine Enables a Converted Person to Serve God with His Mind

Reason, as an instrument of humanity's rebellious nature, can be used for selfish purposes and can be destructive. Upon conversion to Christ, the mind gets a new center and a new set of guiding categories. Thus reason can be used, for example, to check on false claims to revelation. First John 4:1 tells us to try the spirits. First Thessalonians 5:21 states that Christians are to prove all things. Mindlessness is not a Christian virtue. In a time when religious experience and highly emotional religious emphases are in the forefront, there is an important place for the proper use of reason.

## Christian Doctrine Can Enable the Christian to Sort Out Religious and Philosophical Alternatives

In our world of modern travel and communication, non-Christian religions and dynamic philosophies and world views are competing for the allegiance of the world's peoples. Idolatries and dangerous ideologies are especially active in the United States. For example, religious groups that have their origin in the Far East, especially India, have attracted many young adults. A well-known example is Transcendental Meditation, a Hindu devotional cult. This group has attempted to get into the curriculum of public schools and colleges as a help to drug addicts and alcoholics. Transcendental Meditation is presented to Americans under the guise of a religiously neutral form of psychological theory. However, it obviously has roots in classical Hindu religious thought. Also numerous psychological self-help systems which are less than Christian are being promoted.

Secular alternatives, such as Secular Humanism, are advocated. Marxism, with its large following, appeals to humanity's basic economic need but is openly opposed to Christianity.

We are told that the Treasury Department trains agents to recognize counterfeit money by having them examine numerous samples of genuine money. They look at it, feel it, and examine it in great detail. They are thus able to immediately recognize bogus bills. Similarly, if we understand correctly the authentic teachings of Christianity, we can sort out and evaluate false doctrine.

## Christian Doctrine Can Provide Principles for Hard Ethical Choices

These choices are related to questions of abortion, euthanasia, ecology, and energy. There are also questions related to racial and ethnic justice, poverty, hunger, and war. It is not always possible to draw a straight line from Christian doctrine to particular stands on these questions. But Christian doctrine can point in the direction where answers reflecting the Christian world view can be found. As will be emphasized later in this study, Christian doctrine provides a guiding standard and method for interpreting and applying biblical teachings.

## Christian Doctrine Can Be a Vehicle for Teaching the Deeper Meaning of the Gospel

In our contemporary age, it is important, for example, to know what Paul meant by the "righteousness of God" as taught in Romans. John Calvin wrote his famous *Institutes of the Christian Religion* to teach new Christians some of the depths of the gospel. Such deep teaching is an urgent need in what some have called the "Superficial Age" in Christian circles.

### Bibliography

Erickson, Millard. *Christian Theology,* Vol. 1. Grand Rapids, MI: Baker Book House, 1983.

Holmes, Arthur F. *Contours of a World View.* Grand Rapids, MI: Wm. B. Eerdmans, 1983.

Keeley, Robin, ed. *Eerdmans' Handbook to Christian Belief.* Grand Rapids, MI: Wm. B. Eerdmans, 1982.

Ramm, Bernard. *The Evangelical Heritage.* Waco, TX: Word Books, 1973.

Smart, James D. *What a Man Can Believe.* Philadelphia: Westminster Press, 1953.

Wells, William W. *Welcome to the Family: An Introduction to Evangelical Christianity.* Downers Grove, IL: InterVarsity Press, 1979.

# 3
# The Basic Sources for Christian Doctrine

A house is no stronger than its foundation. Before we seek to erect the scaffolding, we must clearly identify and describe the basic building blocks or sources which make up the foundation of Christian doctrine.

Concern in Christian circles about the question of sources or authority usually focuses on three areas. The first source is the Bible. The second source is the teachings and writings of the Christian communities throughout history. The third source of Christian doctrine is the context of the time in which the doctrinal system is formulated. The religious experiences of the people involved in writing and studying doctrine are also important, although tested by Scripture.

## The Foundation Stone: The Bible

### Ultimate and Practical Sources of Theology

The *ultimate* source of all theology is the Triune God in self-revelation. From Adam to Moses, there was no written authority—only the living God in self-revelation. The earliest Christians had only the Old Testament and the remembered oral words of Jesus for a short period.

But soon there were the Gospels, Epistles, and other New Testament books. And so from early Christian history until today, the *practical* authority for evangelical Christians is the Bible certified or sealed to us by the Holy Spirit. In fact *evangelical Christianity* refers to that version of Christianity which places the supremacy and authority of the Word of God for all doctrine over all human philosophies or religions. Obviously, then, evangelical Christians come to the Bible from a confessional standpoint. They hold that theology must find its foundation stone in the Scriptures of the Old and New Testaments. The sixteenth-century Protestant Reformers called this the principle of Scripture alone. Christian doctrine through the centuries is a helpful resource but not the source. Scripture alone as the ultimate source of doctrine separates conservative Christians from others.

In order to emphasize the primacy of the Bible, such phrases as "a fully trustworthy rule of faith and practice" are used. When Christian tradition and human experience are used as resources, they are to be subject to the Bible.

### Special or Particular Revelation

The theological foundation of the doctrine of the Bible is the biblical teaching concerning the special or particular revelation of God in history. There is common grace or a universal revelation of the glory and purpose of God through the created world, reason, and conscience. Sin has warped this universal revelation.

In view of this human condition, God has entered into our world of time and space and both acted and spoken to redeem the human race. In the Book of Exodus, for example, God liberated the Hebrews from Egyptian slavery. God also spoke to his people through Moses to interpret the meaning of his act.

The New Testament tells of the facts of Christ's birth, life, death, and resurrection in actual space and time. It tells of his ascension and second coming and gives an inspired interpretation of the meaning of these facts.

### God's Special Revelation Adjusted to Humanity's Limitations

In the sixteenth century, John Calvin emphasized that God adjusted to humanity's limitations what he wanted to reveal to humans of his glory and salvation. Despite these adjustments to our limitations and sin, the special revelation is sufficiently clear. If there are errors in understanding this revelation, it is the result of our sin not the lack of clarity of the Bible. In faith, and with the help of the Holy Spirit, the simplest mind can know all that is necessary for saving faith and ethical living. And yet the most learned and devoted scholar can never fully search out the depths of all the mysteries of God's revelation.

### Inspiration

Closely related to special revelation is inspiration. This doctrine teaches that God's Holy Spirit so acted on the chosen writers that they recorded exactly what God intended. This inspiration was not mechanical. The biblical writers used the ordinary language, literary forms, and personal background of their day. Nevertheless, God chose to convey his Word through their words. The effect of God's inspiration on these men put them more fully in possession of their own powers of intellect, emotion, and will. The fact that the Word of God came to us through individual human authors even enhances the Word for us. As human beings, we can more readily understand it.

The Holy Spirit helps us to know what God tells us in the Bible. He was the Mover in the writing of revelation and is the Illuminator in the heart of the believer. The Word and the Spirit intersect in the heart of the Christian to create a true knowledge of God and bring into being the Christian principle of authority.

As we shall see, the biblical doctrines of creation and stewardship provide the proper background for technical science. But the Bible is not a book of technical physics, chemistry, astronomy, or geology. The Bible is primarily to be used for the redemptive purpose of mission and action for which it was designed (2 Tim. 3:15-16).

### The Canon or Accepted List of Biblical Books

Because sin has warped our human reason and conscience, we must look to the entirely trustworthy Bible as the basic source for Christian doctrine.

The thirty-nine books to be included in the Hebrew Old Testament were clearly defined and recognized by AD 90. Christians also see God at work in an invisible way in creating the New Testament group of twenty-seven books. The churches recognized God's true Word speaking in and through certain pieces of Christian literature. Step by step, the books which were stamped with apostolic authority were separated from the many materials of secondary importance.

Two basic guidelines, from a human perspective, caused the acceptance of certain books and the exclusion of others. In the *first* place, a book had to come from the circle of early apostles. These were eyewitnesses or associates of the eyewitnesses of Jesus in his earthly life. A *second* guideline called for books which had been regularly read in the churches since the beginnings of Christianity. Later writings had a noticeable spiritual and intellectual inferiority. By the late fourth century, the churches recognized in a more formal manner the twenty-seven books which now make up the New Testament.

In the period between the close of the Old Testament and the time of Christ, the Apocryphal and the related Pseudepigraphical (books written under assumed names) books were widely read and used for doctrine. These books contain substandard materials. They were also widely used in the Middle Ages and are still used by the Roman Catholic Church. The Protestant Reformers, Luther and Calvin, in the sixteenth century, rejected their use for doctrine and used only the Hebrew canon of the Old Testament in imitation of Christ and the apostles. Evangelical Christians continue to follow this policy and use only sixty-six books for doctrine. The other books are used for historical background purposes.

The inspired, canonical books as we now have them constitute Christian authority for ethical living and doctrine. The Bible books are primarily witnessing texts. Christians thus interpret the Bible in light of what it claims to be—a book of witnesses to the revelation of God. One must go through the written Word of God to find out about God and his purposes and salvation. The Bible, as it now stands, is the basic witness to revelation. The Bible is the Word of God written. The Bible is taken up into the life of the churches in each generation by the Holy Spirit (Eph. 1:17-18).

### Translations of the Bible

In regard to translations of the Bible, for serious study, conservative Christians, in addition to the King James Version, use translations such as the *New American Standard Bible, New International Version,* and Revised Standard Version. Paraphrases such as *The Living Bible* are not suggested for doctrinal study. For deeper study, comparing two or more translations is helpful. The newer translations disagree in some places, but none of these disagreements undercut major doctrines.

One important characteristic of evangelical Christians and churches is the supremacy of the Bible. Evangelical Christians often disagree about how to interpret the Bible or on the terms to be used in definitions of the inspiration of the Bible. However, they agree that the Bible is crucially important as God's authoritative and inspired Word and thus the foundational source for Christian doctrine.

## Christian Doctrine Through the Centuries: A Resource

As we have seen, Protestant and evangelical Christians believe that the content of revelation was fixed with the formation of the canon of the Bible. Protestants reject the Roman Catholic teaching that some approved interpretations and teachings of the church after the time of the apostles are as authoritative as the revelation which comes from the apostolic circle. The Protestant Reformers reacted strongly when the medieval church used tradition to justify beliefs and doctrines not found in the Bible, especially numerous traditions concerning the virgin Mary and the purpose of the sacraments. The Roman Catholic Church, on the other hand, continues to maintain the authority of traditions which they claim were handed down orally from the apostles. But the majority of these supposedly apostolic traditions were obviously later in origin.

## Protestant Reaction to Medieval Tradition

In reaction to the Roman Catholic view on tradition, some Christian groups disregard the entire history of the efforts of sincere Christians to understand the Bible and frame Christian doctrine. We now recognize that it is impossible for any group, however informal, to exist for a period of time without tradition. Christian faith normally spreads from person to person by being passed on by tradition. Most of our grasp of the Christian faith reaches us this way.

Tradition, in the best sense of the word, is the Christian faith handed down to us by our spiritual forebears. To despise them and imagine that we can start again as if they never existed is foolish. We listen humbly and respectfully to the voice of tradition. Of course, we are finally subject to the written Word of God. We must test each tradition by the Word of God. Despite the value of tradition, Evangelicals will be careful to maintain the position that no tradition or interpretation possesses the same authority as the Bible itself.

Through the centuries, Christian groups have sought to hear God's Word and interpret it with the Holy Spirit's help. This means that, in formulating Christian doctrine in our time, we must take seriously the work of theologians throughout Christian history. Without this understanding of what has happened before, we become theologically shallow, spiritually weak, blind to the work of God in others, and married to our own culture. In fact, historical theology makes us more self-critical and more open to evaluation of our own preconceptions.

## The Importance of Doctrinal Statements of the Past

All Protestants and Evangelicals, for example, are indebted to the sixteenth-century Protestant Reformers (Luther, Calvin, Melanchthon, Zwingli). Even though these leaders made a radical break with the views of medieval Roman Catholicism, they did not separate themselves from the basic theology of the key leaders of the early church. It should also be noted that the sixteenth-century evangelical Anabaptists (in contrast to the heretical Anabaptists), such as Balthasar Hübmaier who made Christianity personal, did not make it individualistic in terms of disregarding the main teachings of Christian doctrine. Instead, Hübmaier attempted to show that his teaching concerning the necessity of a personal conversion experience, the regenerate church, rigorous moral discipline, and evangelistic and missionary zeal was apostolic and was held by certain key groups in Christian history.

These examples emphasize that the work of Christian theologians throughout history must not be disregarded as a resource for Christian doctrine. Many Christians throughout the centuries have passed on to us the results of their own struggle to hear and translate the meaning of the Christian way in the thought forms of their day. This rich heritage includes the doctrines of the great councils, the piety of the early fathers, the Augustinian theology of grace, the zeal of the monastic reformers, the devotion of the practical mystics, and the integrity of the Christian humanists. This heritage continued in the attempts of the Puritans and Pietists to complete and perfect the Reformation. The doctrinal heritage was reaffirmed by the Wesleys and the Evangelicals. These groups help us learn the whole meaning of Christianity. They add a new angle of vision and enrich our understanding of Christian doctrine.

## Truths to Be Learned from Theological Crises

We should also remember that great theological crises forced theologians to think more deeply and clearly than they do under normal circumstances.

*The doctrine of God and the Trinity.*—In the second century, the Christian churches were faced with the crisis of heresy. This crisis forced them to establish a "rule of faith" or a simple statement of doctrine for those making a first profession of faith. The churches also tried to exclude teachings that were not in keeping with authentic Christianity.

During the third and at the beginning of the fourth century, the churches found themselves divided over the precise nature of God. No one questioned the doctrine of the unity and uniqueness of God. But when Christians confessed that Jesus Christ was God's Son, they seemed to endanger this doctrine of God's oneness. The problem, therefore, was how to express monotheism (one God) in a distinctly Christian form.

A heresy forced a council. A leader in the church of Alexandria, Egypt, named Arius, argued that since the Father "begat" the Son, the Son must be a part of the created order. His line of reasoning went as follows: the Son may be the first of all creation, and he may have an absolute preeminence; that God may have created the world through the Son; but the Son is a created being distinct from the Father. This theology of Arius threatened to split the church.

The Roman emperor Constantine called a council of bishops which met in the city of Nicaea in 325. Their task was to find a way of affirming the deity of Christ without denying the unity of God. This council was held under the leadership of Athanasius. The council concluded that the solution of Arius was unsatisfactory. If the Son of God is part of the created order, then Christians who worship him are idolatrous. And if the Son is not God, then he cannot be the self-revelation of God. Finally, if Christ is not God, he cannot have accomplished the redemption of the human race.

After a period of debate, the Council of Nicaea reached agreement on how to express what has since been known as Trinitarian monotheism. The council stated that God is indeed one, but not simply one. His very being is complex in three distinct ways. He is the Father, Son, and Holy Spirit throughout eternity. The word *Trinity* which came out of these discussions is not a biblical word but an invented word which tries to guard both the unity of God and his complexity. The theological statement produced by the council laid the foundation for the Nicene Creed. This creed has helped all orthodox Christians to guard the doctrine of God since that time by affirming clearly both the unity and the threefold complexity of God's nature.

*The nature of the person of Christ.*—The second major doctrinal dispute which confronted the early church concerned the nature of Christ. Heretics, such as Nestorius, questioned the unity of Christ's person. The

Council of Nicaea had stated that Jesus Christ was indeed God himself. However, it did not deal with the question of how it is possible for God and man to be joined in one being.

A council was held in Chalcedon in 451, and various points of view were considered and condemned. In a positive statement, the council stated that Christ did indeed have two natures. This means that he was both truly God and truly man. But he was only one person. The union did not join God and a man. Rather, this union united, without blending, the divine nature and human nature in one person. In the incarnation, the eternal Son of God took upon himself all that is truly human.

Not all agreed with the Council of Chalcedon. However, the church as a whole continues to hold the Chalcedonian statement about the person of Christ.

These decisions regarding the nature of God and of Christ are among the most significant ones made by the church during those early centuries. These creeds used the language of their time, but they do state basic Christian convictions in a systematic form. Evangelicals today still use the ancient creeds, such as the Nicene and Apostles' Creed, to express basic Christian doctrines.

*The nature of salvation.*—Martin Luther's break with the Roman Catholic view of the place of human works in salvation caused him to probe deeply into the doctrine of salvation. The story of Luther's religious crisis is dramatic and has been told often. In 1505, at the age of twenty-one, Martin Luther made a hasty decision to become a monk. He later became a priest. As he celebrated his first Mass, a service which was intended to assure him of God's forgiveness, Luther was overwhelmed with a sense of his own unworthiness. He began to question the whole of the medieval system of sacraments. Finally, Luther discovered in the Bible the peace with God that had escaped him since he entered the monastery. In the Book of Romans, he read of what he described as the "righteousness by which through grace and sheer mercy God justifies us through faith." Luther stated that he felt that he had been reborn and that he had found that peace through Jesus Christ which he had not found through the accepted system of sacraments.

Luther also stated that salvation is a personal reconciliation with God himself. As an expression of his love, God offers salvation and reconciliation freely. The offer is not dependent in any way upon a person's ability to meet God's demands. Indeed, since people are totally incapable of fully meeting God's revealed standard, his offer of salvation must of necessity be a gift. Luther established a central teaching of evangelical Christianity which is that one is justified by grace through faith in Jesus Christ.

The medieval Roman Catholic theologians defined faith as giving mental approval to the doctrines of the church. In contrast, Luther came to see faith primarily as trusting in a personal God. Of course, a person must have some knowledge about the object of trust. But mere intellectual knowledge of God or mere approval of a doctrinal statement is not enough.

Luther also changed the concept of priesthood. According to Luther, Christians do not need to go through a priest or the saints in order to speak with God. Christians have direct and immediate access to God himself through Jesus Christ. No other intermediary is necessary. This doctrine of the priesthood of believers also means that all Christians are called by God to act as priests to other members of the body of Christ.

These doctrines taught by Luther disrupted the external peace of all Western Christendom. As Luther studied and taught, he came to see the deeper implications of these biblical doctrines. By 1520 he was willing to take on the whole Roman Catholic Church, including the pope himself, in order to purify the church of false doctrine.

*The nature of religious authority.*—John Calvin, the second great Protestant Reformer, questioned the entire Roman Catholic view of the authority of the pope and oral tradition. The Roman Catholic Church had agreed that the Bible is one of the church's most cherished possessions. Ultimate authority, however, rests in the church which authenticates the Bible to individual Christians and guides interpretation. Luther and Calvin disagreed and said that the Bible is self-authenticating. When believers read the Bible, the Spirit speaks through the text and assures them that the message comes from God. It is true that the church formed the canon, but this was merely a recognition that the Bible is the Word of the Spirit.

The church bears witness to the fact that the Bible speaks with the authority of God himself. But the church cannot give this authority. The authority of the Bible does not depend in any way upon the decision of the church; the church must stand beneath the Bible's authority. In this crisis over authority, both Luther and Calvin gave us profound and helpful material on religious authority and biblical interpretation. Unfortunately, Luther was not systematic in his theological work. Calvin, in contrast, belonged to the second generation of the Reformation. By building on the work of both Luther and Zwingli, Calvin was able to construct the first truly systematic expression of Protestant theology.

*The meaning of baptism and church-state relations.*—Another crisis in the sixteenth century concerned baptism. Evangelical Anabaptists stated that only adults were baptized in the New Testament and that the ordinance of baptism always signified a desire to repent. The baptismal rite did not bestow salvation. It was rather a public confession of faith. Since infants are not capable of trusting Christ and since baptism accomplishes nothing in the absence of faith, there is no reason to baptize infants.

The evangelical Anabaptists also stated that the state should have no power over the internal affairs of a local church; and in particular, they repudiated the use of force in religious affairs. The state did have the right to force minimum moral standards, but it should not demand the level of holiness expected within the church. The Anabaptists did agree with Calvin that church members should live outstanding Christian lives. They sought, however, in contrast to Calvin, to accomplish that goal by using church discipline rather than political discipline for those people who did not live up to the high standards.

*The implications of Third-World developments.*—In recent years, there has been a crisis in the so-called Third World (southern hemisphere countries, some Far Eastern countries, and minority and ethnic groups). The Third-World groups have reacted to Western colonialism. This reaction has forced leaders of missionary work to realize that much of our theology in the West is colored by Western Anglo-Saxon thinking and Western economic and social views. In fact, most theology in the West has been written by Americans or Europeans who are white and male. Liberation, black, feminist, American Indian, and Asian types of theology have developed largely as a corrective. Some of these theologies are extreme in their reaction to Western theology, but they should be taken into consideration in formulating Christian doctrine in the late twentieth century. These new theologians point out examples of Christian groups of the past which justified slavery by using biblical texts and saw woman as a "weaker vessel" who was misbegotten and less rational than man. They would oppose these views.

## The Importance of Evaluation and Criticism

As already mentioned in my statements of appreciation of the work in Christian doctrine in past centuries, the priority of the Bible must be carefully guarded. The material we use from the creeds, church fathers, councils, and theologians is always a secondary source. This historical material is tentative and subject to revision.

This process of criticism of historical theology is especially important when the Christian faith is restated or even modified under the influence of a powerful philosophy which the church seeks to use in stating doctrine. The Roman Catholic Church, for example, is greatly influenced by the fact that their theologians sought to use the philosophy of Aristotle in the late Middle Ages. In our particular time, experience-centered and scientifically oriented philosophies have been offered as frameworks for reinterpreting the whole of the Christian faith. Evangelical scholars point out that these reformulations tend to water down or even cut away some of the crucial features of the Christian gospel.

A new development in our time is the spread of the occult and Far Eastern world views, especially in the United States. In some cases, these groups are attempting to restate Christianity in such a way as to change its basic meaning. Although we cannot ignore the context of each age in which Christian doctrine is written, we must be alert and not allow the context to dominate the Christian faith.

We also must recognize that some of the doctrinal statements in Christian history have been colored by religious hatred and poor understanding of the Bible. Even the more balanced and significant ecumenical creeds and Reformation doctrinal statements are conditioned by history and culture. Nevertheless, in our twentieth-century formulation of doctrine, we will use the history of doctrine as a resource, always evaluating it by the truth of the Bible as the Bible is certified to us by the Holy Spirit.

## Cultural Setting and Religious Experience: The Context

The third basic building block or source for Christian doctrine is the present cultural setting and religious experience—the context. Evangelical Christians have had difficulty with the manner in which this approach has been used and is being used. In the 1950s, there was the existential theology of Bultmann and Tillich. Next there was the political theology of the 1960s and the liberation theology of the 1970s. In order to call attention to a neglected area, some of these new developments have overemphasized one aspect of Christianity. Evangelical leaders seek to form a theology which addresses the life situation of our time without losing balanced biblical substance or essence. Conservative leaders, such as Carl Henry, state that evangelical theology must be creative. It is unworthy if it is only repetitious. But in seeking contemporary relevance, Evangelicals must be faithful to historic biblical beliefs.

### Doctrine and Contemporary Thought Patterns and Issues

In order to be meaningful, Christian doctrine must be formulated in the thought patterns of our age. This includes the use of the language forms and frameworks of the thought of our time. For example, how can we talk about God being up there (transcendent) and down here (immanent) in our time? The problem is presented by the fact that modern physics and astronomy say that space is curved and there is no "up there" in the ancient sense. Karl Heim, a well-known German theologian, and others state that we should talk of God as being in another dimension that is not fully open to us in this limited earthly life. Other theologians who emphasize the future orientation or focus of the Christian faith restate the transcendence (beyondness) of God in terms of God being the pull or the lure of the future. God is described as out in front of history pulling history in his direction. God is also seen as out ahead of history in terms of time, in anticipation of where history ought to be going. In this way, God can give us the clue to what we should be doing.

There is also the problem of how we can talk about the demonic (demons) in the light of the contemporary understanding of subconscious forces operating on human personality. Christian psychiatrists, such as Paul Tournier, believe that there can be a helpful joining of Christian teaching and insights from psychology.

Doctrinal teaching should also relate to living issues, such as ecology, economics, war, family life, and abortion, as well as to general doctrinal matters. We should not just deal with the questions of the past age or repeat the statements of another era. Rather, Christian theology should seek to bring new awareness of the meaning of Christian doctrine to our day. This does not mean a surrender to the modern mind-set; it means a restatement of the biblical message in a way that communicates with our generation.

## Awareness of Secular Influences and Personal or Group Interests

Culture is significant in its influence on doctrine. In most theological systems, strong evidence of the influence of secular teachings can be found. Cultural views and even political views help to shape doctrine. In some cases, nonbiblical ideas, such as dualism which sees nature and the body as evil, are influential. This dualism has become so noticeable that a group of evangelical leaders and scholars from different backgrounds gathered together to issue The Chicago Call to Evangelicals to restore and restate the balance of historic Christianity. The Chicago group stated that the tendency of Evangelicals to understand salvation only as an individual, spiritual, and otherworldly matter, to the neglect of the communal, physical, and this-worldly implications of God's saving activity, should be recognized and given up. Evangelicals were urged to recapture a view of salvation and the Christian life that embraced the balanced and comprehensive biblical view.

In some cases, Christian doctrine is constructed in such a way as to further personal or group interests. The Protestant Reformer John Calvin left room in his writing for both the conservative and revolutionary approaches to the problem of the rights of civil rulers. There is strong evidence, however, that his interpretation of the Bible and doctrinal formulations were weighted in the direction of magnifying the power and place of civil rulers and magistrates. There is also evidence that this emphasis was at least partially caused by a reaction to the revolutionary and nonconformist views of the radical Anabaptists of his time. The radical Anabaptists protested some aspects of Calvin's church-controlled state in Geneva, Switzerland, and stirred up unrest in Europe. In reaction, Calvin emphasized portions of the Bible, such as Romans 13, which teach that the Christian is to be subordinate to those in authority.

One of Calvin's most devoted disciples was John Knox of Scotland. He went to Geneva to be with Calvin after he was forced to flee Scotland because of unrest and a non-Protestant ruler. Eventually, Knox returned to Scotland where Queen Mary, a Roman Catholic ruler, opposed Protestant teaching. She was both powerful and headstrong. There seemed to be no orderly way to gain freedom for Protestant preaching and practices. Knox decided to help organize a movement to remove her from the throne. He was reminded that Calvin had taught that the Christian is to be obedient to those in power. Knox replied that Calvin's interpretation was formulated in response to the radical Anabaptists. Therefore, Knox, to meet his different practical situation, sought out those portions of the Bible that called for open opposition to a government or ruler who would not allow freedom to preach the Protestant faith. This is an excellent historical example of how equally devoted people differ and argue over the interpretation of the Bible and the formulation of Christian doctrine. The differing approaches of Calvin and Knox were influenced by the practical and personal interest needs of particular situations.

In recent years, the youth leaders, who opposed middle-class culture, and those concerned with ecology have used the Bible as a philosophical basis to protest what they think is a wrong and selfish approach to nature and natural resources. They point out that the Bible teaches that any subcreating humans do is *under* God, for God's glory and humanity's good, and not for private financial gain. These leaders also seek to emphasize that Jesus was more of an itinerant prophet than an industrialist. They point out that Jesus stated that the foxes had holes and the birds had nests but he had no place to put his head. These anti-middle-class leaders further note the interest of Jesus in small children, women, and the down-and-out. They add that Jesus was not particularly concerned with material things. Noting these emphases of Jesus, it is not surprising that these same leaders have adopted Francis of Assisi as their model. Francis rebelled against middle-class values and his father's business and returned to the simplicities of nature.

Thus the Bible and Christian doctrine are used to undergird two different approaches to nature. Two groups take the same passages of Scripture and disagree in its meaning for doctrine. Each group finds the Bible meeting its own particular, practical need or interest.

### Recognition of Developments in Society and Personal Prejudices

Although there are other factors involved in millenial (Christ will rule for a thousand years) doctrine, changes in society have influenced the approach taken toward the meaning of the millennium. *Postmillennialism,* which teaches that there will be a "golden age" established upon the earth by the supernatural powers of the gospel preceding the return of Christ was widely held in the early 1900s. Eminent orthodox leaders, such as B. H. Warfield, B. H. Carroll, and George W. Truett, taught that

Christ would not return to earth until *after* the golden age—or millennium—had been established upon earth.

This postmillennial teaching was shaken by two world wars, a worldwide depression, and the incarnations of satanic evil which the present generation is witnessing. To take its place as a popular view, there arose among conservative scholars a doctrinal teaching which is called *dispensational premillennialism,* or *pretribulationism.* This new view arose out of a prophetic awakening in the early nineteenth century in England under the leadership of John Nelson Darby. Darby was very disillusioned by the deadness and formalism of the Anglican Church and its ordained ministry. He taught a doctrine which was pessimistic about the advance of the kingdom until the return of the Jews to Israel and the reign of Christ with his saints from Jerusalem. As for Christendom and the church in general, Darby taught that God had already forsaken them. Believers in dispensational doctrine were to either leave the mainline apostate churches or seek to bring as many people within them as possible to true prophetic understanding. In most cases, they should assemble in simple unity in informal Bible churches.

Many factors were involved in the development of Darby's viewpoint. However, cultural and social factors in Darby's England—and later in the United States—undoubtedly influenced the popularity of this dispensational understanding of Christian doctrine.

In the light of these examples, it is important that Christians should not import unexamined influences from the world into Christian doctrine without benefit of close examination and criticism. Influences coming from our personal experience or cultural influences always present a clear and present danger of distortion. The student of the Bible and doctrine, therefore, should utilize every possible safeguard in the pursuit of the ideal which is listening to the message of Scripture without mixing in his or her own unexamined and admitted prejudices.

It is especially important to be self-conscious of the influences which have formed and influenced us. This conditioning is subtle, and we often mix up our own view of doctrine with certain secular cultural values. In contrast to the dispensationalists already discussed, some existentialists or experience-oriented theologians emphasize the here and now so much that they leave little room for a future-oriented theology with its sense of urgency and hope in the second coming of Christ and its strong sense of the power of evil in history.

**The Necessity of a Limited Relationship to Culture**

Of course, there will necessarily be a limited relationship to culture, but there should not be a wholesale adaptation to culture. This limited relationship to and knowledge of contemporary culture will help to make doctrine intelligible to those to whom it is addressed. In other words, doctrine must be connected to the realities of our time and place.

It is also true that theology must use some intellectual framework or philosophy to formulate doctrine. Whenever a person reads a statement of Christian doctrine, he must also look for the philosophy which was utilized in its construction. Every theologian is to some measure also a philosopher. The basis of this assertion is that theology, done in the proper way, involves assumptions, categories, tests, concepts, and forms of logic. These materials are derived from philosophy. An example is the way in which Thomas Aquinas, an important theologian for Roman Catholicism in the Middle Ages, used Aristotle's philosophy to formulate his system of Christian doctrine.

**Religious Experience and Doctrine**

*The Protestant Reformation.*—As indicated in the discussion of the evangelical Anabaptists, a source and confirmation of Christian doctrine is individual Christian experience. Both Luther and Calvin framed Christian doctrine and interpreted or rediscovered the Bible in the light of their personal experience with Jesus Christ. No true understanding of God is possible without a trust relationship with God himself through Jesus Christ.

*The Great Awakening.*—This same emphasis was characteristic of the Great Awakening in the United States in the 1740s. In a manner reminding us of the Protestant Reformation, this period of religious revival placed importance on personal conversion which involved a personal faith in Jesus Christ. Those who disliked the revivals held that one could grow up in a church and come gradually to a Christian commitment without going through a conversion experience. Those who felt that conversion should be part of every Christian's experience supported the Great Awakening. Today, some two hundred years later, this stress on personal experience is an important element in the doctrinal statements of evangelical Christianity.

*John Wesley.*—John Wesley also made an important contribution to

American evangelical life in the eighteenth century. He was ordained in the Church of England. In 1735 he came to the United States. Soon he returned to England without having achieved notable spiritual results because he himself had not yet experienced spiritual rebirth. Wesley told the story that, after returning to London in 1738, he attended a small chapel meeting at which Luther's *Preface to the Book of Romans* was read. According to his own report, his heart was warmed during the reading, and his conversion that night transformed his whole life. He traveled throughout England preaching the Word of God with great power among the people of Great Britain until his death in 1791. His theology emphasizing the importance of personal conversion has become a major element in doctrinal history.

*The Pentecostal or charismatic movement.*—In contemporary religious life, experience is playing an important role in the continuing discussion concerning the formulation of Christian doctrine. The Pentecostal movement has taken the stand that speaking in tongues is a needed outward sign of the inward filling of the Holy Spirit. This movement also states that other evidences of the presence of the Spirit, such as gifts of healing or prophecy, are also possible in the twentieth century. The individuals who experienced this Pentecostal power formed denominations in which their distinctive theology could be freely taught.

The early Pentecostals thought of themselves as fundamentalists (extremely conservative in doctrine). Fundamentalists, however, as a whole, were not open to their teaching. Most fundamentalists were advocates of a dispensational theology which teaches that the special gifts of the Spirit, such as tongues, healing, and prophecy, belong solely to the Apostolic Age, not to the present age. So, for many years Pentecostals were not accepted in conservative Christian circles.

After about 1960, however, Pentecostal theology gained well-trained supporters within both the mainline Protestant denominations and the Roman Catholic Church. This recent activity is usually called neo-Pentecostalism or the charismatic movement. The term *charismatic* comes from the Greek word *charismata* which means "gifts." The explosive growth of the Pentecostal or charismatic movement has forced the larger evangelical community to restudy and evaluate again this relatively new emphasis in doctrine.

Followers of charismatic theology state that they have noted a scriptural truth which the church has systematically and intentionally ignored. They also contend that the extensive experience of twentieth-century Pentecostals justifies their teaching that the baptism of the Holy Spirit is real and that all of the gifts of the Spirit mentioned in the Bible are available to Christians today. Fully convinced by their own experience, they tend to see those who oppose their teachings as resistant to the work of the Holy Spirit.

On the other hand, evangelical theologians who are not charismatic have tended to deny that charismatic theology is truly biblical. They disagree with the charismatic interpretation of the Bible. They also insist that personal experience alone must never be allowed to determine doctrine. As a result, the zeal of the charismatics has frequently met with an equally zealous rejection by many conservative Christians. Many congregations in the United States have split over this issue.

In recent years, however, discussions have occurred; some reconciliation seems to be taking place. Many charismatics have recognized that it is unbiblical to insist that all Christians speak in tongues. The larger evangelical community, meanwhile, has begun to recognize that God has used the baptism-of-the-Holy-Spirit movement to arouse interest in the doctrine of the Holy Spirit and the biblical concept of spiritual gifts. In our systematic discussion of the Holy Spirit, more will be said about this continuing discussion and its influence on formulating a doctrinal system which will include a balanced emphasis upon the Holy Spirit and spiritual gifts.

### The Priority of the Bible Over Experience

In relation to the place of context and experience as a source of doctrine, as well as in relation to historical doctrinal statements, Evangelicals insist that context and experience be interpreted in the light of the Bible. This is in contrast to those who insist that personal religious experience is what really counts as a source of doctrine. Evangelical Christians, however, state that the Holy Spirit who convicts and regenerates Christians and who inspired the Bible never contradicts himself. The Christian experience often illuminates something in the Bible that otherwise might be obscured, but it does not lead a person to doctrines or views that are in opposition to the clear teachings of the Bible. This issue will be further discussed in the chapter on the method of interpreting the Bible.

Despite the possibility of misuse, evangelical Christians insist that for the Bible to become meaningful and authoritative for doctrine, its teachings and Jesus Christ, about whom it is centered, must be personally received by faith. However, authority and the personal reception of it should not be confused. We must remember that experience is the means by which we are put in contact with truth; it is not itself the truth. Whatever authority a person attributes to experience is nothing but the truth *mediated* or brought to him by the experience.

Despite a strong emphasis on doctrine, the Protestant Reformation was not just an effort in intellectual discussion and research. It was experience and life. Calvin stated that, through a sudden conversion, God turned and subdued his heart. Calvin was captured. He renounced himself to follow Christ and stated that he had offered his heart as a sacrifice to God. Evangelicals continue to agree that the Christian life consists not merely of an intellectual acceptance of a doctrinal statement, a commitment to attend church on Sunday, or a desire to establish casual social relationships with other Christians. Rather, Evangelicals emphasize the necessity of a personal commitment to Jesus Christ which leads them by his power to seek to become like him.

The Chicago Call to Evangelicals states that Evangelicals suffer from a neglect of a balanced personal spirituality on the one hand and an excess of undisciplined spirituality on the other hand. According to this group, we have too often pursued a so-called superhuman or ultra-pious religiosity rather than the biblical model of a true humanity released from bondage to sin and renewed by the Spirit. This group also called for a rediscovery of the devotional resources of the whole church, including the evangelical traditions of Pietism and Puritanism. We need an exploration of devotional practice in all traditions within the church in order to deepen our relationship both with Christ and with other Christians.

Thus we see that personal Christian experience is crucial in formulating and appreciating doctrine. But we have also seen that we must not make our personal experience an unconscious norm or standard for building doctrine. Rather, the Bible must illuminate and interpret our experience. The widely reported experiences of God's people through the ages can also help us avoid taking something that is peculiar to our individual experience and raising it to a necessary standard or norm. We should avoid the "If you didn't get it like I got it, then you ain't got it" approach.

## The Importance of Balance in Using Resources for Doctrine

All Christians would agree that we must have sources for Christian doctrine. The three basic sources have been outlined. But it is also obvious that these sources can be misused. The fact that we emphasize that the Bible is the final source can result in a wrong type of worship and use of the Bible. This approach would cut the Bible off from the other sources. On the other hand, there are some who are impressed by the carefully defined statements and power of creeds, councils, bishops, and various Christian communities. This group would insist that the church alone is to be heard on ultimate matters. This results in an improper emphasis on the church as a doctrine-defining institution. In some cases, the secular world and mystical religious experiences are allowed to define doctrine; the Bible and the historic Christian formulations become marginal. This is *secularism* (human-centered approach) or a non-Christian mysticism. It is important, therefore, for the basic building blocks or sources for Christian doctrine to be seen and maintained in proper balance and priority.

### Bibliography

Coleman, Richard J. *Issues of Theological Conflict.* Grand Rapids, MI: Wm. B. Eerdmans, 1972.

Davis, John Jefferson, ed. *The Necessity of Systematic Theology,* 2nd ed. Grand Rapids, MI: Baker Book House, 1978.

Fackre, Gabriel. *The Christian Story.* Grand Rapids, MI: Wm. B. Eerdmans, 1978.

Fackre, Gabriel. *The Religious Right and Christian Faith.* Grand Rapids, MI: Wm. B. Eerdmans, 1982.

Johnston, Robert K. *Evangelicals at an Impasse.* Atlanta: John Knox Press, 1979.

Keeley, Robin, ed. *Eerdmans' Handbook to Christian Belief.* Grand Rapids, MI: Wm. B. Eerdmans, 1982.

Menendez, Albert. "Who Are the Evangelicals?" *Christianity Today,* January 27, 1978, p. 42.

Ramm, Bernard. *Pattern of Authority.* Grand Rapids, MI: Wm. B. Eerdmans, 1957.

_____. *The Evangelical Heritage.* Waco, TX: Word Books, 1973.

Wells, William W. *Welcome to the Family: An Introduction to Evangelical Christianity.* Downers Grove, IL: InterVarsity Press, 1979.

# 4

# The Guiding Key: The "Already-Not-Yet" Stream of Redemptive History Centered in Jesus Christ

On a trip to the People's Republic of China, we had a brilliant guide who had been a member of the Communist party many years. He pointed out to us that Communism, based on the teachings of Marx, Lenin, and Mao, is the key to understanding history, past and present. Communism is also the key to what he called a "spiritual materialism." The guide had studied the little Red Book of Chairman Mao's sayings as his bible. Communism, he said, gave him power for the present and hope for the future of his people.

Christian doctrine, in a far more profound, truthful, and vital way, has a guiding key in the already-not-yet stream of redemptive history centered in Jesus Christ. This guiding key will be explained fully after examining the alternative keys. Briefly it means that *already,* in the first coming of Jesus Christ, the spiritual blessings and power of God are made available. However, evil and Satan are active, and so Christians eagerly look forward to the second coming of Christ and the age to come when the fullness of the spiritual blessings of God *not yet* available will be given to us.

## Alternative Statements of the "Key" in Christian History

At different times and at different places in Christian history, leaders have proposed guiding keys which would help people understand the Bible and develop Christian doctrine. A number of keys have been suggested. For example, the idea that Jesus Christ fulfilled in his person the concern of the ancient Greeks for a "Universal Logos or Word or Pattern" in the universe helped to relate Christianity to the thought world of the early Christian centuries. This key is emphasized in John 1:1-14. A significant contribution of the Protestant Reformation was its emphasis on the fact that the Bible is to be interpreted in accordance with its central theme. For the Protestant Reformers, there was a central truth in the Bible that acts as a base for interpretation. Luther found this key in the Pauline concept that man is made right with God through faith in Jesus Christ (justification by faith), especially as this teaching is given by Romans and Galatians.

Many New Testament scholars recognize that the Old Testament, the writers of the first three Gospels, the apostle Paul, and most of the other New Testament writers were oriented toward the future or the age to come. Scholars, such as Albert Schweitzer, stated that the kingdom of God is to be seen primarily as something that will come when Christ returns. Reacting to the future emphasis, a group of scholars argued that the mind of Christ in Paul concerning the future was gradually replaced by an emphasis on the Christian's present spiritual unity with Christ. This key suggests that one gains most of the new riches of divine grace in the present spiritual relationship with Christ.

The search for a key to understand the Bible and formulate Christian doctrine has led others to use a current philosophy as a framework or vehicle to restate Christian doctrine. For example, in the thirteenth century, Thomas Aquinas used the philosophy of Aristotle. In the twentieth century, some theologians are using the thought of Alfred North Whitehead and Martin Heidigger as vehicles for restating doctrine. Others find help in formulating a key from some dominant cultural emphasis, such as Harvey Cox's secular gospel and a liberation emphasis.

## The Importance of a Guiding Key

In light of the alternative suggestions, we need a key or guideline which reflects the dominant biblical emphasis. Such a key is important because of the complexity and richness of the Bible. The proper key can function as a principle of selection, organization, and drawing together of the biblical materials and Christian doctrine. This key should not impose itself on the biblical materials but should flow from the Bible as its source.

## The All-Embracing Nature of the "Already-Not-Yet" Key

### The Statement of the "Key"

All of the keys suggested as guidelines to formulate doctrine have some validity. But these keys do not embrace enough of the emphases of the

Bible. The key I am suggesting includes the truths mentioned in the other keys. As we will see, this key includes both theory and practice.

Any adequate key must have a future orientation if it is to be true to the Bible. An emphasis on the age to come pervades the Bible. The Old Testament is the inspired record of divine activity in history in which God initiated and carried forward his purposes for humanity's salvation. The purposes of God have been and are being accomplished in history past and present. And yet, in the Old Testament, the great purpose of God is future.

In the New Testament, a different orientation is found. But the element of expectation and hope remains and is still dominant. The *full* experience of realities of redemption and salvation remain for the future. They are "not yet." However, salvation is no longer merely an object of future hope. The totality of the Christ event includes his life, teachings, death, resurrection, and ascension. God has entered into human history to bring certain future salvation realities into *present* experience.

The New Testament describes the entire sweep of human existence in terms of this age and the age to come. In the first coming of Christ, the blessings of the future age have been made available for human enjoyment. However, the present age continues to experience negative forces because Satan is active and powerful. The Bible repeatedly says that the fullness of redemptive blessings awaits the glorious appearing of the age to come. The main emphasis of the Bible, therefore, is that the age to come is always an object of hope and expectation.

We see, therefore, that the most fruitful way in which to state the key to understanding the Bible would be in terms of a combination of the future emphasis and the present redemptive history emphasis. I will, therefore, use the phrase "the already-not-yet stream of redemptive history centered in Jesus Christ" as the key for our study of the Bible and as the basis for constructing Christian doctrine.

### The "Key" Illuminates and Reveals the Unity of the Bible

*The key and the Old Testament.*—Israel's God was radically different from the pagan gods in the ancient world. The sharpest contrast was that the pagan religions were keyed to the rhythm of nature and were nonhistorical. Israel's faith, on the other hand, had a lively sense of history. Israel's God worked through the events of history to accomplish his redemptive purpose. In fact, Israel saw her history as the special place where God was working out his redemptive purpose. Of course, redemptive history is not all there is to Old Testament and biblical faith. But the major emphasis of much of the Old Testament is that Yahweh (God) had acted, was acting, and would act in Israel's history for her salvation.

The redemptive history emphasis in the Old Testament is seen in terms of the basic features of the Old Testament. *One feature is election.* Everywhere one looks in the Old Testament, one encounters the conviction that God in his gracious purpose called Israel to himself, delivered her from bondage, gave her the Promised Land, and made her his chosen people.

*A second feature is the concept of covenant (sacred agreement).* In fact, Israel first emerged into history as a covenant society. When the fugitive Hebrew slaves who had experienced the Exodus deliverance at the Red Sea entered into covenant with God at Mount Sinai, a new society was formed where none had been before. The people of Israel acknowledged that they were nothing until God, in his gracious acts, delivered them from slavery. In gratitude to him, they accepted him as their divine Lord and made a sacred agreement to live with one another under his overlordship in gratitude for his redemption.

The covenant renewal ceremony was at the heart of the life of Israel. The later histories of Israel were written to show the extent to which the nation honored or dishonored their obligations to the covenant.

In the later parts of the Old Testament history, especially with the coming of the prophets, the concept of redemptive history became even more prominent. The prophets challenged the people in the light of God's covenant and dealings with them in the past. They predicted the doom of Israel (the ten northern tribes) and Judah (the two southern tribes) if the people did not maintain the covenant.

A *third feature* of the Old Testament is a *confident hope for the future.* Confidence in what God would do in the future can be observed in the very earliest period in Israel's history. The theme of the promise, moving on to fulfillment, dominates the thought of the Old Testament as it tells the story of the patriarchs, the Exodus, the wilderness wandering, and the giving of the land. Promise for the future is built into the very nature of the covenant of Sinai itself. If this covenant imposed strict requirements, it also carried with it the assurance that, if its demands were met, God's favor would be endlessly continued.

With the classical prophets (Isaiah, Jeremiah, Amos, Ezekiel, Daniel), the promise was pushed farther into the future as they began to look into the age to come. In the immediate future, the prophets saw judgment and not promise. However, beyond the catastrophe, they looked for the time when God would once more rescue his faithful people. This hope took many forms. There was the expectation of an ideal king of David's line or the reestablishment of the covenant of Moses on a new and deeper level. In Ezekiel, there was a promise of a national resurrection and a confirmation of the covenant with David. Other parts of the Old Testament record a promise of a new exodus march out of the wilderness of Exile and the turning of all nations to God. Daniel saw the coming of the Son of man on the clouds of heaven. Thus we see that a dominant characteristic of the Old Testament is its forward look and its hope based on the promises and power of God.

The ruin of the nation of Israel (the captivity), although it broke the hearts of the prophets of God, did not crush their faith. God, who had judged his people, was also the one who had shown mercy on them in Egypt. They looked for a future deliverance.

The Old Testament forms a redemptive history with an orientation to the future. Remembering the record of God's great acts of old, the Old Testament closes in anticipation of greater acts of God. Thus, the Old Testament is an incomplete redemptive history book. It is a book in which hopes are often dashed and at best only partially realized.

The nation of Israel was destroyed in a geographical sense. Yet Israel as a people of faith survived. She still looked forward with heightened intensity to God's deliverance in the future. Down to the end of the Old Testament period, Israel looked for the fulfillment of God's promise. Down to the last prophet, the Old Testament speaks of the fulfillment of promise in the future tense.

The New Testament affirms that the promise made in the Old Testament has been fulfilled. The long-awaited salvation event and the turning point of all history has taken place in Jesus Christ. The God who acted in Israel's history has acted decisively in Jesus Christ. Where the Old Testament anticipates, the New Testament announces. It has happened. As Mark 1:15 states, "The time is fulfilled, and the kingdom of God is at hand." Jesus Christ is the Messiah, the promised deliverer of David's line. He is also the servant of God, and he has done his sacrificial and saving work and now is exalted to the highest heaven and will one day come again to bring into being the final stage of his kingdom.

*The key and the New Testament.*—A presentation of representative examples of how the already-not-yet theme of redemptive history illuminates and brings together New Testament materials should be helpful.

The kingdom of God had started its work among the Pharisees (Jewish religious leaders) by virtue of *Christ's deeds and work during his earthly ministry* (Luke 17:20-21). Jesus also talked of the future when he would die on the cross as a ransom for many and then be raised from the dead. This was to be an even more decisive and greater coming of the kingdom. Jesus finally described the day when the Son of man would come in glory to bring his kingdom to victory (Matt. 25:31 *ff.*). The kingdom among people began with the activity of Christ in his public ministry, but its fullness would only come in the age to come. In other words, in his public ministry, Christ was beginning to fulfill and accomplish his redemptive purpose. More was to come. It was *already* but *not yet*.

*The signs and miracles of Jesus* pointed to the work of the kingdom. The statement of Luke in 11:20—"But if I with the finger of God cast out devils, no doubt the kingdom of God is come upon you" (author's translation)—is related to the plagues of Egypt, which were wrought by the finger of God. The plagues were the beginning demonstrations of power pointing forward to the decisive act of God in the Exodus itself. By relating his exorcisms (casting out demons) to the finger of God, Jesus was placing them in the same relation to his own exodus, which, during his ministry, still lay in the future. His acts, comparable to the Old Testament Exodus, were the cross-resurrection event, the pouring out of the Holy Spirit, and the second coming. The exorcisms of Jesus were the beginning assault on the kingdom of Satan. The cross, resurrection, and the final overthrow of Satan at the end of history would complete the assault.

*The parables of Jesus* illustrate the mystery of the kingdom. The concept of mystery has an Old Testament background in the Book of Daniel, where divine secrets were disclosed to men. In the New Testament, mystery is a disclosed or open secret, the revelation of the divine purpose. It was no secret that God would one day establish his kingdom in glory and triumphant power—this was orthodox Jewish theology. The mystery is that the kingdom which is to come finally in outward power, as foreseen in Daniel, has, in fact, entered into the world in advance in a secret form to work quietly within the lives of human beings. This is a mystery, a new revelation.

Each of the parables in Matthew 13 illustrates the mystery of the kingdom. This mystery is that the kingdom of God which is yet to come in outward power and great glory was actually present among people in advance in an unexpected form in the ministry of Jesus. This unexpected presence in advance is for the purpose of bringing to people in the present evil age the blessings of the age to come. The parable of the mustard seed illustrates the truth that the kingdom, which one day will be a great tree, is already present in the world in a tiny, insignificant form. The Jews could not understand how the coming glorious kingdom could have anything to do with a movement so insignificant as that of Jesus and his disciples. Jesus answered: first a tiny seed, later a large tree. The future form of the kingdom is not to be measured by its initial insignificance.

The one point in the parables of Matthew 13 is that with the coming of the Messiah, the kingdom began. From a human perspective, this seems to have been an insignificant beginning. Yet it was not at all insignificant (Matt. 13:31-32). The parables of the treasure and of the pearl teach that the kingdom, though appearing in a new and insignificant form, is yet the most valuable treasure in the world and is to be sought at all costs (Matt. 13:44-46).

This, then, is the mystery of the kingdom. It comes quietly, humbly, without fire from heaven, without a blaze of glory, without a rending of the mountain or a cleaving of the skies. It can be rejected by hard hearts; it can be choked out; its life may sometimes seem to wither and die. But it is the kingdom of God. It brings the miracle of divine life to humanity. It introduces the blessings of the divine rule. It is to those who receive it the supernatural work of God's grace. And, this same kingdom, this same, supernatural power of God, will yet reveal itself in a more dramatic form at the end of the age, purging all sin and evil from the earth.

We can use the already-not-yet key when reading *the Gospel of John*. For example, eternal life, like the kingdom of God, belongs in its fullness to the age to come (John 14:3). But eternal life, again like the kingdom of God, has become an object of present experience (John 3:36). In both cases, the anticipated future has entered into present spiritual experience. As the doctrines of eternal life and the resurrection involve both present and future, so John teaches that judgment is both a future separation at the last day and a present spiritual separation between persons based upon their relationship to Christ (John 3:18-19).

The coming of the Holy Spirit, recorded in *the Book of Acts,* at Pentecost is another example of God continuing to act redemptively in history. The Holy Spirit temporarily overcame the separation of nations divided by language. But the Spirit will completely dominate the future kingdom of God. The miracle of Pentecost is that the Spirit moved down into this old, sin-corrupted creation in the present age, even though it does not completely transform its outer framework. The miracle of Pentecost occurred primarily in the church creating a realization of a fellowship in Christ carried out by the Spirit of God, which is a foretaste of that which is to come (Acts 2:1-11).

Peter's speech at Pentecost (Acts 2:14-21) was based on the prophecy of Joel. Since the Spirit had laid hold of the community, the kingdom of God was being realized by people, at least in a preliminary way. The apostle Paul called the Spirit that already exists in the present the firstfruits (Rom. 8:23) and an earnest or down payment (2 Cor. 1:22). By this Paul was stating that the Spirit represents the part of the future kingdom that is already working in the present.

*The ministry and writings of Paul* can be examined with the already-not-yet key. The redemptive history approach even throws light on Paul's doctrine of justification. Through faith in Christ on the ground of his shed blood, believers have already been justified, acquitted of the guilt of sin, and delivered from condemnation (Rom. 3:24-26). The age to come has moved back into this age. Justification, which belongs to the age to come and issues in future salvation, has become a present reality. The age to come has reached back into the present evil age to bring its salvation blessings to those who believe.

The doctrine of adoption also finds its completion in the realm of the future kingdom. While we have entered into the Christian relationship as children of God and have received the spirit of adoption which accompanies that relationship, the fullness of adoption is still future. On the contrary, while we enjoy the firstfruits of the Spirit, we groan inwardly as we await the adoption, the redemption of our bodies (Rom. 8:23). The enjoyment of our inheritance as sons and daughters is incomplete apart from the final fulfillment when the firstfruits will be followed by the fullness of harvest and the transformation of the body in the resurrection. Apart from the final day, the doctrine of adoption is incomplete.

The redemptive history, already-not-yet key also throws light on 1 Corinthians 7:29-31. Paul wrote that, because of the urgency of the time, believers should not permit themselves to become too involved in this world order. "For the form of this world is passing away" (v. 31). Paul did not mean to indicate that the world is evil in itself. A life of physical detachment or asceticism is not required. The structure of worldly relationships is, however, transitory and destined to pass away. Since Christians belong to the new divine order, while they still find themselves in the world and must make use of the world, the goal of life must not be that of finding their deepest enjoyments and satisfactions on the worldly level.

## Conclusion

Thus, we have attempted to give examples of how the already-not-yet redemptive history key throws light on difficult and controversial verses and passages in the Bible and reveals the basic unity of both the Old and New Testaments. In setting forth a viewpoint, undoubtedly an overemphasis has been made in certain places. Nevertheless, it is still the central task of biblical and doctrinal study to seek that which is the guiding key. My conviction is that the already-not-yet theme of redemptive history centered in Jesus Christ is the key which is most in keeping with the central emphasis of the Bible and, therefore, should be dominant in Christian doctrine.

### Bibliography

Beasley-Murray, George R. *Preaching the Gospel from the Gospels.* London: Lutterworth Press, 1956.
Bright, John. *Authority of the Old Testament.* Nashville: Abingdon Press, 1967.
Cullmann, Oscar. *Christ and Time.* Philadelphia: Westminster Press, 1950.
Cullmann, Oscar. *Christology of the New Testament.* Translated by Shirley C. Guthrie and Charles A. M. Hall. Philadelphia: Westminster Press, 1959.
Ladd, George E. *The Gospel of the Kingdom.* Grand Rapids, MI: Wm. B. Eerdmans, 1959.
Ladd, George E. *Jesus and the Kingdom.* New York: Harper and Row, 1964.

# 5
# The Guiding Method: The "Historical-Overarching" Approach to the Basic Source

We began our study with the conviction that the Bible is the basic source for Christian doctrine. The next concern is related to the method of understanding and interpreting the Bible and its basic message. The problem of the proper method of biblical interpretation is not only a concern of pastors and professional Christian workers but is also a major concern of laypeople in the churches. This concern surfaced at a retreat for a large group of laypeople in New Mexico. They suggested three categories of problems. First, what are the basic principles of biblical interpretation? Second, how do you utilize these principles to make the Bible and its message relevant in a contemporary world which is quite different from the ancient biblical world? Third, as evangelical Christians, how do we interpret the symbolic or figurative or poetic parts of the Bible?

These laypeople were saying that as Christians they wanted to become informed and responsible participants in God's redemptive purpose as set forth in the Bible. Furthermore, they wanted to understand the Bible so that they could seek to make their life-world conform to the teachings of the Bible. However, to some extent, they are outsiders to the Bible's language, thought patterns, and cultural and historical ideas. They wanted to know the process by which they could read the Bible as insiders.

The same concern surfaced at a major conference on the Bible which met at Oxford University a few years ago. This conference agreed that it has always been the task of the church to unfold the message of the Bible. The Oxford conference concluded that developing specific principles of biblical interpretation is crucial. The participants were surprised to find that there was general agreement on *four basic principles* of interpretation: the *grammatical, historical, theological,* and *practical* principles of biblical interpretation. Some will suggest variations of arrangements, wording, and order; but the principles will be essentially the same. These principles have been accepted by most Christians in the evangelical tradition.

The advantages of utilizing these principles are many. This approach exercises some control over interpretation. A check is placed on the temptation of the interpreter to seek out hidden or foreign meanings in the Bible. Furthermore, the grammatical-historical-theological-practical approach has proved itself through the years. Scholars, pastors, and laypeople who follow these principles have made constructive and abiding contributions to Bible knowledge and understanding.

In using these principles, we should not just repeat past doctrinal statements. Rather, we should seek to grasp afresh, with creativity and imagination, the basic theological message of the Bible for our time.

### First, Understanding the Words and Thought Forms of the Bible

*Grammatical Principle*

From the method by which any type of literature is interpreted, there arises the grammatical principle. The Bible is written in human languages. The Bible is a historical product. Although the Bible is divinely inspired in its final origin and essential content, it was written by men in human language and under human relationships. The first step is to interpret the Bible with similar helps and according to the same principles as other books from ancient times.

The Bible is a book which communicates information through words. Thoughts are expressed through the relationship of these words. Each individual word contributes something to the whole of the content expressed. The better we understand the individual words used in biblical statements, the better we will be able to understand the total message of Scripture.

Laypeople often complain that theologians use too many big words. Scholars tend to develop a technical language within their field for the sake of precision not confusion. Our everyday language is used in such a broad way that our words take on meanings too elastic to be useful in precise communication. We can see the advantage of technical language in the medical field even though we are sometimes annoyed with it.

**Allegory (Hidden Meanings)**

Some Christians, as well as cultic groups which parade as Christians, bypass this concern for grammar and the common-sense meaning of words. They use what is called the *allegorical* method of interpretation.

In allegory, foreign elements or ideas are read into a word, thereby assigning it a so-called "deeper" or "spiritual" meaning. The original or straightforward meaning is often ignored or even denied outright. In allegory the natural sense of a passage may well be given up intentionally. The chief goal of the allegorical interpreter is to seek to discover hidden meanings.

The allegorical method flourished in the Middle Ages. There was little concern for the grammar of the Bible. The Bible was generally interpreted without regard to historical background. There was a general ignorance of the biblical languages (Hebrew, Greek, Aramaic). Bible translations were not precise and clear-cut.

Bible verses were said to have two, three, and four meanings. *Jerusalem,* for the medieval interpreters, could refer to the literal city in Palestine or, allegorically, to the church. Morally, it could refer to the human soul. The word *sea* could mean a gathering of water, the Bible, the present age, the human heart, the active life, the heathen, or baptism.

The search for hidden meanings became so extreme that a premium was placed on the unusual and the surprising. Augustine, in the fifth century AD, found interpretations fruitful in proportion to their unusual or difficult nature. For example, the ark was seen as the figure of the church which was rescued by the wood on which Christ hung. The dimensions of the ark represented the human body in which Christ came. The door in the side of the ark signified the wounds in the side of the crucified Christ.

In more modern times, men like Emanuel Swedenborg and groups like Unity and Christian Science have utilized allegorical interpretation.

Christians should base serious study of Scripture on a good text—the original language or a careful translation—and quote it accurately. Of course, no translation of Scripture is without its problems. Some passages have been unusually difficult to translate, let alone fully understand. But most of the Scripture is relatively straightforward.

**Poetic and Symbolic Passages in the Bible**

Each type of literature in the Bible should be understood in the light of its own literary type. In straightforward narrative, words are taken at face value. In poetic sections, a different approach is needed. Fortunately, the Revised Standard Version and certain other modern translations indicate which parts are formally poetic in the way in which the Bible is printed.

Jesus said, "If your right eye causes you to sin, pluck it out" (Matt. 5:29). Was he suggesting self-mutilation? Obviously this verse must not be interpreted in a literalistic way. Jesus often used hyperbole (exaggeration for a purpose) and figurative language to stress truth. Herod was called "that fox" (Luke 13:32). Paul referred to James and Cephas as "pillars [in the Jerusalem church]" (Gal. 2:9). The word *pillar* must not be taken to refer to a shaft of masonry work. The literary context makes clear that James and Peter were dependable leaders of the church. Peter described the devil as a roaring lion (1 Pet. 5:8). Metaphoric or poetic language must be recognized as such. Look for the reality and truth taught through the medium of dramatic language.

Genuine *symbols* are not simply bare images. They present truth in a lively manner. When John the Baptist said, "Behold, the Lamb of God, who takes away the sin of the world!" (John 1:29), he was employing symbolism. Neither the original hearers nor the readers of the Bible today imagine that he was talking about a four-legged, woolly animal. But those who know something about the Old Testament sacrificial system and have knowledge of the Christian gospel understand the symbol of the Lamb.

In one sense, much of biblical language must be *figurative* or *poetic*. If it is to be meaningful at all, biblical language must, as Thomas Aquinas pointed out, be analogical (use earthly comparisons). Most biblical statements are neither wholly like nor wholly unlike their point of reference. Jesus Christ and the lamb do have a genuine similarity. Jesus Christ, in an important way, was related to the sacrificial lamb of the Old Testament sacrifices. Yet there is a difference between the man Jesus and the animal called a lamb.

Other examples could be given. The Bible states that God is our

Father. This, of course, does not mean that in the human sense God has marital relations with a woman and helps to bring children into the world. And yet there is some analogy between the way I relate to my sons, if I am a good father, and the way the Heavenly Father relates to the Christian. There is a clear parallel or analogy here.

Again the Bible states that God is the rock of our salvation. This means that as a rock has stability, so has God. The Bible describes God as one who has arms. This indicates that as human arms have power, so God has power.

The Old Testament book, the Song of Solomon, furnishes us with another example of the Hebrew use of analogy or comparison. It tells of a young lady who has a neck like the tower of David (Song of Sol. 4:4). If one were to take that description literally, the picture of such a girl would be ridiculous. Obviously, the writer here was using a picturesque, Hebraic analogy to say that the girl was similar to the tower of David in some way. As the tower of David was beyond the reach of an army, so this girl was beyond being reached for immoral purposes. She was a virgin.

Recognition of the reality behind the poetic or figurative nature of much biblical language helps us in interpreting the biblical accounts of creation and last things. To say that certain language about the second coming of Christ is figurative, for example, does not mean that the event of the second coming is unreal. Earthly language from a known sphere of existence is oftentimes used to describe what took place at creation or will take place in a future sphere of existence that no mere human creature has ever entered. God thus used dramatic or even poetic language to reveal that which took place in creation (before man was in existence) and that which will take place at the end of history.

In Revelation 20:11, God is described as one who is seated on a great white throne. From his face the heavens and the earth vanish or disappear. The very language of God being seated is figurative language. His occupying a throne is a way of describing his majesty. The use of the phrase "from whose face" (literally) helps to show that the God of revelation is a personal being. By this figurative language, the actual, personal being of God confronts the reader. God is the reality whom he will face in judgment.

## The Importance of Context

Doctrinal misunderstandings also arise because people ignore the context (surrounding materials of a verse or passage). Basic to any understanding of a word or verse in the Bible is the context. For a farmer, a donkey means a beast of burden. In the context of a national election in the United States, a donkey means the Democratic Party.

If verses are seen in context, difficulties in interpretation have a way of solving themselves. The "work out your own salvation" phrase in Philippians 2:12 makes sense if seen in context. It is a call to concern for the welfare of others as God's design for the deliverance of the Philippian church from a threatening disunity (compare Phil. 2:1-5; 4:2-3). In this context, Paul did not mean that one's personal salvation is based on one's good works. That would be contrary to the biblical teachings and to the evangelical doctrine of salvation by grace through faith, not by works.

The Book of James, with its emphasis on good works, and the Book of Romans, with its emphasis on salvation by faith, are sometimes said to contradict each other. Seen in context, however, they actually supplement each other.

We must remember that the New Testament Epistles, from a historical and human perspective, are specific first-century letters written out of the context of the author to the context of the recipients. An analogy could be a situation in which we are listening in to one side of a telephone conversation and seek to piece together from this one side what the other party is saying or what his problem is. Our difficulty is that we are removed from the New Testament writers by time, circumstances, and culture.

Being aware of the context of a passage in the Bible involves attention to three types of context. First, there is the immediate context of the passage. Second, there is the larger context of the whole book of which the passage is a part. Third, there is the intellectual and cultural framework of the entire Bible seen from the earliest Old Testament revelation to the closing of the New Testament age over a thousand years later. This means that good Bible students will spend their whole lives without exhausting the task of seeing each biblical passage in its threefold context. But as you study carefully, year by year, you will find yourself getting a better and fuller sense of these three types of context improving your scriptural and doctrinal understanding.

The leader of the Hindu-based Transcendental Meditation movement, Maharishi Mahesh Yogi, has taken a Bible verse out of the biblical context and moved it over into the context of his Hindu world view. He interprets "Be still, and know that I am God" (Ps. 46:10) as meaning that each person should meditate and come to the realization that he is essentially the godhead itself. This scriptural verse has a particular meaning when taken within the intellectual and broadly cultural framework of the Bible itself. The Maharishi has lifted it out of that context and placed it within the frame of reference of the Hindu system, thus giving it a different meaning.

## Second, the Original Historical
## Background of the Bible

Many so-called "spiritual" or "pietistic" groups neglect the second basic principle of biblical exegesis which is usually called the historical background principle. Since the mid-nineteenth century, this principle has been a basic principle used by all serious interpreters. It includes a consideration of the geographical, historical, and cultural background materials related to the Bible. Since God chose to give us his Word through human words in history, it is obvious that it can best be understood in an accurate and complete way if the historical background and particularity of the Bible is studied. Interpreters must seek to creep out of their twentieth-century skins and identify themselves with the feelings and life of the biblical times.

The more critical interpreters who see the Bible primarily as a human book oftentimes allow the historical background and culture to overshadow the actual content being considered. For an evangelical interpreter, the biblical writers are considered to be men of their times, yet men above their times. For both types of interpreters, however, the historical background is important.

If a solid historical base has been established by the interpreter, then historical imagination can be used in applying biblical truths. The imagination of the biblical community deals primarily with images which have come from biblical history. Thus *pharaoh* came to be a symbolic reference to every form of oppression. And the biblical stories cluster around such images, so that every oppression-liberation event is a new dealing with pharaoh.

The imagination of an informed Christian, however, should always be

a historical imagination. It is the capacity to return again and again to
the concreteness of the past of Israel and the church and to see new
meanings there. A historical approach keeps the application concrete
and particular. But a historical approach without imagination tends to
be dry and uncompelling. Imagination, on the other hand, without a
historical base, tends to turn to undisciplined fantasy. There are many
examples of the nonhistorical use of the Bible by cultic groups in our
time.

## Third, Overarching Theological and
## Internal Spiritual Principle of Biblical Interpretation

Evangelicals, in the 1920s and 1930s, reacted to an overemphasis on
the grammatical, critical, and historical principles by some interpreters.
The historical critics succeeded in textual work, grammar, literary history, and archaeology. A great assortment of facts and data concerning
the Bible was analyzed and classified, but they often missed the theological or salvation meaning of the Bible. The theological and practical
principles of interpretation were largely ignored.

### Theological and Internal Spiritual Principle of Interpretation

Interpretation of the Bible is an attempt to discover and describe the
meaning of the biblical books. It can be scientific and authentic only
when it takes seriously the testimony of the biblical writers. The interpreter is not to bring his own ideas to the Bible. The theological themes
confront the interpreter in the biblical material and his method must
recognize their presence.

The primary conviction of the Bible writers was that a gracious God
acted in history in order to reveal himself to sinful persons. The Bible
is the divinely inspired account and interpretation of this revelation in
history. An interpreter must take into account these basic theological
truths. He must be obedient to the nature of the Bible. Sound interpretation must be both historical and theological.

Fortunately, in recent years, new tools, such as theological word
books, have been produced. These studies indicate, for example, that
Jesus was not simply a refined teacher of the Golden Rule and the general
fatherhood of God. Rather, Jesus was accepted as the Messiah who
fulfilled in his life, death, and resurrection the promises of the Old

Testament prophets that God in the fullness of time would act redemptively in history.

The biblical reports do not present external events in a manner satisfactory to the technical classification methods of natural sciences. The writers who were responsible for the Bible were involved in the events and both remembered and interpreted them. What happened and the theological interpretation of those happenings were fused together. The writers were confronted by, overwhelmed by, and found new existence in their encounter with God in Jesus Christ. Jesus was described in the Bible by persons who believed in him as the Messiah. The escape of the Hebrews across the Red Sea was reported by men who remembered, were caught up in the deliverance, and saw the deliverance as God's action.

In many cases, there was a time interval of oral tradition between the biblical events and the literary fixation (writing down in final form) by the biblical writers. The Bible is the result of a complex process of forming, shaping, and growth. This interval of time between events and the Bible as we now have it has not been neutral and vacant. As the biblical events were reported, they gained a new dynamic contemporary meaning. As the events were recited, the witnesses were given deeper revelations of the meaning and implications of the original events, such as the Exodus and the life, death, and resurrection of Jesus Christ.

### The Importance of a Personal Relationship with God

Evangelicals disagree with interpreters who believe the Bible can be adequately interpreted apart from a personal relationship with the God of the Bible. The interpreter of the Bible is not like an experimenter in natural sciences. The interpreter should be aware of his convictions and subject them to the testing of a careful study of the Bible. Of course, all people have convictions in any type of thinking or interpreting. At least the Christian interpreter admits his convictions. The Bible cannot be fully understood from the outside by grammar, logic, rhetoric, and history alone. The Bible's center yields itself best to people who have a personal relationship with God through Jesus Christ and who are indwelt by the Spirit of God.

*Illumination versus Spirit-led interpretation.*—A fine line separates Spirit-led interpretation from illumination. According to the sixteenth-century Protestant Reformers, God originally revealed his Word through the Holy Spirit, but the Word remains cold and distant until the Holy Spirit completes his work in a given person's life. The Holy Spirit must illuminate the hearts and minds of readers so that they can grasp the personal significance of the text. For example, the Spirit may use a particular text to convict people of sin or to draw them to worship. We call this the illumination of the Bible by the Holy Spirit. Evangelicals are in agreement on this concept of illumination.

But Spirit-led interpretation goes one step further. Advocates of this approach insist that the Holy Spirit not only illuminates the hearts of thoughtful readers who use their minds to study God's revealed Word but the Spirit may also speak with readers directly to communicate new and hitherto unrevealed content. Those who believe in Spirit-led interpretation insist that the Spirit speaks directly to the heart and gives additional revelation or content not found in the Bible. This is done without necessarily utilizing the written text of the Bible. And so, according to advocates of this position, readers of the Bible should listen primarily to the Holy Spirit who speaks within them.

This approach is open to serious objections. It tends to make the text of the Bible secondary. It also unnecessarily depreciates the value of the intellect in Bible study. The Evangelical would follow the concept of illumination and reject a Spirit-led interpretation.

### The Importance of the Analogy-of-Faith Approach

As has been noted, some Christians practice the arbitrary selection of Bible texts to undergird an ethical view or a doctrine in which they are interested. Other texts equally important but inconvenient to or contrary to the view or result desired are passed over, played down, or artificially harmonized. Slavery, for example, was defended on biblical grounds as divinely ordained, or at least permissible.

Proof-texting (using isolated Bible verses), as well as allegorizing (seeking hidden meanings), was widely practiced in the Middle Ages. To counteract this approach, the Protestant Reformers in the sixteenth century developed the analogy-of-faith principle of interpretation. This is sometimes called *doctrinal interpretation.* The Bible is to be interpreted in accordance with the analogy of faith which is the substance of Scripture doctrine found in the plainest passages of Scripture. In other words, Scripture is to be its own interpreter. Stay with the main and plain teachings of the Bible.

Before we list the more practical aspects of the analogy-of-faith approach, it should be helpful to list some fundamental ideas upon which it is built.

*First, the Bible is unified.*—Though a wide diversity of styles, perspectives, and cultural settings is found in the Bible, this diversity is held together by a unified theology.

*Second, the Bible is coherent* (it holds together).—Diversity does not destroy coherence if there is a dominant unifying principle. We have found this principle in the guiding key in chapter 4.

*Third, the central teaching of the Bible is clear.*—This conviction led to the insistence in the Protestant Reformation that the Bible should be translated into the languages of the people and thus made available to laypeople. The principle of clarity does not teach that all parts of the Bible are equally clear. It recognizes that some portions of Scripture are obscure and difficult to interpret. Rather, the principle of clarity calls attention to two essential points. First, the central message of the Bible is clear enough for the unskilled person to understand. The message of salvation in Christ is not obscure. Second, what is obscure in one part of Scripture is often made clear in another part. Not taking the whole of the Bible into consideration has resulted in the rise of many cults that claim to get their teachings from isolated parts of the Bible.

*Fourth, the Bible is inspired.*—The assumption of inspiration requires and demands the analogy of faith. If the Bible is inspired by God, then to set one part of it against another is to make God speak with a forked tongue. In fact, the ultimate test of a person's view of the Bible is found in his method of interpreting it.

#### Four Practical Aspects of the Analogy of Faith

*First, the New Testament is the key for interpreting the Old Testament.* —Once we grasp the overall arrangement of the Bible and see that it is a book of promise and fulfillment, we will always look to see how the New Testament interprets the Old Testament. For instance, God promised Abraham a seed which would bring a blessing to all nations. The New Testament interprets that seed as Christ and the followers of Christ (Gal. 3:6-16; Rom. 4:11,16).

Some people pride themselves on being able to understand Old Testament prophecies if they simply take them "literally." And without consulting the interpretation of the New Testament, they arrive at all sorts of fantastic things which are supposed to happen in modern-day Palestine. A prophecy may or may not be meant to be understood literally. For example, Isaiah declared that God would put a foundation stone in Zion, one that would support a building in time of wind and hail (Isa. 28:16). Isaiah did not say that he meant that the stone is a person. It is a veiled prophecy of Christ. We need the New Testament to interpret it for us (1 Pet. 2:6-8). Prophecy is not self-interpretive but should follow New Testament insights. The New Testament fulfills the Old Testament.

Not only does the New Testament show us how to interpret the prophecies of the Old Testament but it also shows us how to interpret the laws of the Old Testament. The New Testament shows us how the Old Testament laws of ceremony have met their spiritual reality in the person and work of Christ. But not all the laws found in the Old Testament are ceremonial in nature. Some are moral, and these moral principles still bind the Christian. The apostle Paul referred to a number of them as a rule of life for Christians. The Sermon on the Mount interprets the moral teachings of the Ten Commandments, and Jesus strengthened their demand for holiness (see Matt. 5:17-28).

The New Testament accepts that part of the moral law in the Old Testament which is in continuity with the teaching and meaning of Christian doctrine. The New Testament transforms and perfects Old Testament moral mandates in the light of Jesus Christ. Some of the Old Testament regulations (for example, ceremonial laws) were rejected by the New Testament in the light of the new standard established by Christ.

The New Testament shows us that it is not correct to view the Old Testament as if it were on the same level as the New Testament. The Christian is not to defend slavery, the owning of concubines, polygamy, or similar culture-bound practices. The eye-for-an-eye ethic which persists in certain forms of criminal justice and in war-making was set aside by Christian teachings. The harsh (nonredemptive) attitudes toward sexual sins must be modified to conform to the redemptive attitude embodied in Christ's ministry. Emphasis on moral judgment must be balanced with divine mercy and compassion. In other words, the Bible is to be understood from its center—its heart—its Christ. The Old Testament is the book of preparation and the New Testament is the book of fulfillment.

But it should be remembered that Christian doctrine, although finding its norm in Christ and the New Testament, does build on the Old Testament. Crucial Old Testament emphases are on God's holiness and on human accountability for violating God's holy laws. The moral rigor of the Old Testament is important in Christian ethics. The New Testament, especially the apostle Paul in Romans 9—11, refuses to disqualify Israel from a continuing role in God's purposes.

*Second, systematic or clear sections of the Bible should have priority for doctrine over passages where the teaching is incidental or unclear.*—An example of this emphasis is seen in the doctrine that a person is made right with God (justified) by faith in Jesus Christ and his life, death, and resurrection. This doctrine is treated in a systematic teaching form in Romans and Galatians. It is only common sense to affirm that these books where justification by faith is a central concern should be the primary guides for discussion of this doctrine. Bible passages where this teaching is mentioned in an incidental way should be looked at in the light of places where the teaching is clear. This approach is actually the kind of procedure which educated people follow when any body of material or system of thought is under examination.

Major heresies (nonorthodox teaching) are often the result of turning a minor reference into a major doctrine. In 1 Corinthians 15:29, for example, Paul made a reference to "baptism for the dead," (author's translation). Most scholars admit that Paul's meaning here is obscure. But the Mormons use this as a scriptural basis for a complex doctrine of baptism on behalf of dead people. According to Mormon doctrine, the authentic priesthood and authentic salvation were lost to those who lived between the death of Mormon in the fifth century AD and the time of Joseph Smith, the discoverer of the writings of Mormon and restorer of true salvation, in the nineteenth century. Baptism for the dead (by proxy) can assure salvation for those who died before the authentic priesthood was restored.

A closely related principle is one that affirms that major doctrines should not be founded on one verse or a few miscellaneous verses. Rather, the main teaching or emphasis of the Bible, especially the New Testament, should be sought. A major doctrine should be founded on much Scripture. Inevitably there will be aspects of biblical truth that appear to finite minds to be contradictory, such as human freedom and God's determining power. A reverent Bible student will accept both of these truths although they appear to be in conflict.

To refer to the 1 Corinthians 15:29 passage on baptism for the dead, we must remember that a major doctrine must be taught clearly and undergirded by numerous examples. It is precisely for this reason that one must reject the Mormon application of 1 Corinthians 15:29. The analogy of Scripture does not allow us to regard such a practice as either required or repeatable by later Christians.

*A third emphasis states that the historical narratives in the Bible are to be interpreted by the teaching passages.*—Much of Paul's writing is instructive in character. The relationship between the Gospels and the Epistles has often been defined in the simple terms of saying that the Gospels record what Jesus did and the Epistles interpret the significance of what he did. Such a description is an oversimplification, but it is true that the emphasis in the Gospels is found in the record of the events of the life, death, and resurrection of Jesus. On the other hand, the Epistles are more concerned with interpreting the significance of those events in terms of doctrine, exhortation, and application.

Since the Epistles are largely devoted to interpretation and come after the Gospels in order of organization, the Protestant Reformers maintained the principle that the *Epistles should interpret the Gospels* rather than the Gospels interpret the Epistles. This rule is not absolute but is helpful.

Since the loss of confidence in biblical authority in our day on the part of some people, it has been fashionable to put the authority of Jesus over against the authority of the Epistles, particularly Paul's Epistles. People do not seem to realize that they are not setting Jesus against Paul so much as they are setting one apostle, such as Matthew or John, over against another. We must remember that Jesus wrote none of the New Testament, and we are dependent upon apostolic testimony for our knowledge of what he did and said.

Thus the principle of interpreting the narrative sections of the New Testament by the teaching sections is not designed to set apostle against apostle or apostle against Christ. It is merely recognizing that a chief purpose of the Epistles was to teach and to interpret the mind of Christ for his people.

One of the reasons why this rule is important is to warn against drawing too many inferences from records of what people do. For example, can we really construct a manual of required Christian behavior purely on the basis of an analysis of what Jesus did? Jesus lived under a different period of redemptive history than contemporary Christians. He chose to fulfill laws of the Old Covenant, including dietary and ceremonial laws. Here is why the Epistles are so very important. They do call for us to imitate Christ at many points. But they help us to find out what those points are and what they are not. That Jesus remained unmarried shows that celibacy is good, but his celibacy does not demand that marriage be renounced by Christians, as the Epistles make clear.

*In the fourth place, each part of the Bible must be seen in relation to the dominant or overarching emphasis of the Bible on God's ongoing redemptive purpose in history.*—God's saving purpose is an unfolding process. Each event in the Bible has its roots in the past, its meaning in the present, and its fulfillment in the future. When the Bible is seen as an unfolding process, the historical portions and the seemingly unimportant events in the Bible have meaning and importance.

The Bible as a whole provides the broad context for interpreting any one of its parts. This means that, if we fence off one area of the Bible (Old or New Testament) and generalize about it in isolation, this procedure tends to lead to imbalance. Christian theology needs to be based on the entire Bible.

While God's activity did not begin with the historical Jesus, it came to its fulfillment in him. Thus God's activity in Old Testament times must ultimately be understood from the standpoint of Christ. One can agree with Luther that all experiences of grace, even those of Old Testament times, are finally to be seen as experiences of Christ. It would be a mistake to try to find direct references to Christ in the creation story of Genesis 1. It would, however, be appropriate (perhaps required) to refer to Christ in discussing the contemporary meaning of Genesis 1 because the creation event of which Genesis 1 speaks is ultimately to be understood in the light of Christ (John 1:3; Col. 1:16).

Indeed, for a Christian, everything of which the Old Testament speaks has to be seen in the light of Christ. But immediately when one says that, one has to add again that everything in the New Testament has to be seen in the light of the Old Testament. For the Christian view is that Jesus is the One on whom the faith of Israel ultimately came to focus. But faith can only be Christian if it is built on the foundation of the Hebrew Scriptures.

Christ is, then, the hidden content of Old Testament history and the revealed content of New Testament history, and so he unifies biblical history.

## The Importance and Usefulness of Typology

An important approach used by Christians in dealing with the Old Testament is called typological interpretation. According to the method of typology, some events or ritual practices in the Old Testament are symbols or foregleams of truths which are clarified (or even events which occur) in the New Testament. The careful interpreter should, therefore, note and point out such parallels between the two Testaments. The method rests on several assumptions: (1) that there is a fundamental theological unity between the two Testaments; (2) that events described in the Old Testament may be historically true and at the same time possess a significance which goes beyond their actual history; and (3) that many concepts and principles which are spelled out in detail within the New Testament are prefigured within the Old Testament.

Typology thus has meaning in a unified view of the Bible which sees it as having an overarching redemptive purpose. In the life and worship of Israel, there was a constant reinterpretation and re-presentation of the original revealing acts of God because God's will and actions were seen as basically the same in every age. At the great annual Jewish festivals of pilgrimage the important events of Israel's history were re-presented.

Israel also looked to the future and saw a correspondence between the future and the past. In Israelite thought, there was a historical analogy or likeness between future events and beginning events. Thus Amos and Isaiah spoke of the return in the last days of the Paradise experience. Amos also looked for the return of David, and Hosea and Isaiah mentioned the return of the wilderness days when God's people did not have to have a king but lived directly under God. These prophets were not simply predicting that a particular historical event would recur. Rather, it meant that a greater one than David would come. It would not be an exact wilderness experience, but a greater deliverance from bondage.

This means that the Old Testament writers saw a continuity of history. It also means that, from the standpoint of the New Testament, we see meanings in the Old Testament that the original authors missed because the coming of Christ illuminates the action of God in Israel. However, one must be careful to make a distinction between typology (likeness, analogy) and allegory (hidden meaning). One should not look for an exact correspondence in details between the Old and New Testaments or seek hidden spiritual meanings. Rather, one must seek historical analogies or likenesses. This approach can be called promise and fulfillment.

Promise is the understanding that God has determined to accomplish his purposes and is already working toward the completion of this goal. Promise is not just a word about something that is to come; it speaks of a future already in progress of fulfillment. The Old Testament pictures God's actions in history as a series of promises (not predictions) and fulfillments, each fulfillment giving rise to the expectation of a greater fulfillment in the future. This is because the promises of God were never exhausted by one fulfillment.

In the latter Old Testament prophets, such as Isaiah and Amos, the final fulfillment of promise became oriented toward the future. This shows that the fulfillments in Israel were only the beginning phase of God's plan. So when Christ came and brought the promises to historical reality, he ensured the validity of the Old Testament by showing that it is part of the same divine program which he fulfilled. Thus the Old Testament is valuable for the Christian churches since Christians are still on the road to the final fulfillment.

The Old Testament experiences of the people of Israel were types or correspondences to the experiences of Christ and the church. What the Old Testament servant experienced (but always with the note of promise for triumph), the New Testament servant, Jesus Christ, experienced (but now in fulfillment). Thus Peter in Acts 2 saw Joel's prophecy of the day of the Lord being fulfilled in his day with the coming of the Holy Spirit. So typology is concerned with historical correspondence. The Old Testament hope of a land, a rest, and long life with physical pleasures becomes the hope of eternal salvation in the New Testament.

An Old Testament event or figure or institution must not be regarded as important only because it provides us with a type looking forward to the New Testament. If this takes place, we miss the meaning and importance that an Old Testament event had in its own context. The application of typology should not limit our use of the Old Testament only to those portions where we can determine clear correspondences to the New Testament. In other words, the Old Testament has value apart from typology.

An example of seeing an Old Testament passage in the light of the overarching redemptive purpose is the Christian interpretation of the

Ten Commandments. Behind the Ten Commandments, there sound the words, "I am the Lord your God, who brought you out of the land of Egypt, out of the house of bondage" (Ex. 20:2). Here Yahweh reminded his people of his grace to them in rescuing them from slavery and calling them to himself. God then, in the Ten Commandments, laid down the terms to which the people had to conform if the covenant bond was to be maintained. Specifically, the people of God were to acknowledge no other god save Yahweh, and they were to live in community with one another and with him in obedience to his covenant law. The Ten Commandments are seen as a description of the conduct required of God's people in response to his unmerited favor, especially revealed in the Exodus.

The saving act of God to which the Christian must in gratitude respond is not one of deliverance from slavery in Egypt but Christ's deliverance from bondage to sin and death. Christ in no way did away with the law but announced its fulfillment. In so doing, Christ radically reinterpreted the law and gave it new depths of meaning (classically, in the Sermon on the Mount). The Commandments of God therefore remain valid for Christians, but their setting has been changed from Mount Sinai and placed in the new theological setting of the covenant given at the cross.

In this light, the law discharges its function as a tutor (see Gal. 3:24) leading us to Christ. Anchored in the gospel, the law leads to the gospel. At the same time, because it has not been done away with but fulfilled by Jesus, the demands of the covenant continue to have significance. They remind us that the response demanded to the grace of Christ is the recognition of Christ's supreme and sole lordship and obedience to his commands in every encounter with our brothers.[1]

### Fourth, the Practical Principle of Biblical Interpretation

Many disagreements arise among Christians in regard to the practical meaning of the Bible. The climax of biblical interpretation is the application of the biblical message to the modern world. Having found out what it *did* mean, the interpreter must ask, What *does* it mean?

The interpreter needs to move from the first to the twentieth century without abandoning the essential meaning of the Bible, on the one hand, and without keeping us back in first-century culture, on the other hand. How can a biblical teaching, spoken to a given historical context in response to a specific historical problem, become the Word of God for us, whose context is so different? How or when does something that is culturally conditioned become transcultural (have meaning beyond the early centuries).

### Practical Contemporary Meaning from Figurative Language

Many examples of the importance of the practical principle could be given. Is God literally on a throne a few thousand feet in the air? Isaiah 6:1 describes God on a throne with a robe and gives some details of his bodily appearance. Utilizing the doctrine of accommodation (stooping down to our condition) suggested by John Calvin over four centuries ago, a contemporary interpreter realizes that the description of God in Isaiah 6 was the way God was represented to Isaiah by the Spirit of God. Behind and through the vision, expressed in eighth-century BC categories, was the truth for both then and today that there is a personal God of holiness at the spiritual center of the universe. For Isaiah, Calvin, and contemporary people of faith, the use of the upward metaphors (God is up above on a throne) to describe God preserves the theological truth of the otherness and beyondness of God. Isaiah's statement will forever prevent any monist (God and nature and humanity are the same) or mystical identification of God and humanity, such as some Hindus and Buddhists teach today.

In Revelation 20:12,15, the dead, the great, and the small, stand before the throne of God. Books are opened. The dead are judged according to their works from the records. The word "book" in Revelation 20:12,15 refers to a scroll. The phrase "the books were opened" refers to a scroll being unrolled. This is figurative language. John stated that all of our names are recorded upon this register of life. This description conveys the idea that God knows well the doings of all people and the destiny of humankind.

If God were to impart the same revelation to a prophet in modern times, some kind of electronic computer might provide the figurative language or metaphor to picture God's records of judgment. But neither scrolls nor electronic computers are necessary for God's judgment. The full reality of God's knowledge and decisions are beyond human description. But however God does it, there will be one result: people will answer to God for what they are, for what they have thought, and for what they have done.[2]

The realities described in the Bible by the figurative language of creation and the last days are crucial for our understanding. This is true because we are deeply involved in the results of creation or will soon be the active participants in judgment.Therefore, we need the use of figurative and literal language to give us every possible insight.

We should interpret figurative language in a way which will cause it to make its full impact upon our contemporaries. We must use these biblical emphases and the eternally valid teachings given by them to confront people with their Creator, their Redeemer, and their Judge.

This dramatic and figurative type of biblical language and the truths conveyed by it were not given to satisfy our scientific curiosity but to assure us about the "whence" and the "whither" of our existence. To let our ignorance of what we do not know become a battleground among Christians while we lose sight of what we do know is most tragic. The urgent message of creation and last things must be heard at all costs, and nothing should be allowed to obscure it.

### Determining Principles in Applying the Biblical Teachings

In most cases, practical application involves the working out from the biblical passage a principle for life today. In this connection, a passage should never be used in such a way as to distort the original meaning. First Corinthians 11:27, according to the King James Version, is translated, "whosoever shall eat this bread, and drink this cup of the Lord, unworthily, shall be guilty of the body and blood of the Lord." The word "unworthily" has caused some individuals to suggest that they are not worthy of partaking of the Lord's Supper.

The Revised Standard Version rendering of 1 Corinthians 11:27 is more in keeping with the original Greek language when it translates the original as "in an unworthy manner." In Corinth, the Christians evidently turned the love feast, which was climaxed by the Lord's Supper, into an orgy or drunken brawl. The meaning of this passage for today is that the Christian should participate in the Lord's Supper in a reverent and worthy manner. None of us are worthy except by the atoning death of Jesus Christ.

Should Evangelicals drink wine? First Timothy 5:23 states an admonition from Paul to Timothy, "Use a little wine for the sake of your stomach." Most Evangelicals state that this admonition was culturally and specifically bound. Water was unsafe to drink, so Timothy was to take wine for medical reasons. However, in light of America's major problems with alcoholism, many Evangelicals believe that other teachings of Paul about the importance of Christian influence in potentially harmful areas should lead Christians to a total abstinence from alcoholic beverages.

Some people try to regulate details of life from specific biblical texts. Conflict arises when the biblical details are not followed. After the original meaning of a passage has been studied, the interpreter is in a position to apply it to life today. But the emphasis should be on principles and not on specific details. The New Testament writers constantly moved through specifics to principles. It is obvious that no one should try to dress or follow the hairstyles of first-century people. Yet the principle of quiet modesty is involved in the biblical materials which deal with dress and appearance (1 Pet. 3:3; 1 Tim. 2:9).

### Determining the Transcultural or Permanent Element in Biblical Teachings

The application of the practical principle constantly forces the interpreter to answer the questions, how does one determine what is cultural and therefore belongs only to the first century? and what is transcultural or permanent and therefore belongs to every age?

It is obvious that some things are clearly culturally conditioned while others are just as clearly transcultural. For example, indicatives and imperatives—such as, "Put on then, as God's chosen ones, holy and beloved, compassion, kindness, lowliness, meekness, and patience, forbearing one another and, if one has a complaint against another, forgiving each other" (Col. 3:12-13)—clearly transcend culture. These are the obvious texts which seem to make the Epistles so easy to interpret.

On the other hand, for Western people the statement by Paul about the eating or noneating of food offered to idols is of little consequence (1 Cor. 10:23-30). The only possible way, therefore, that we can find how 1 Corinthians 9 through 10 speaks to our situation is to translate the first-century situation into the twentieth century. The principle of avoidance of acting as a stumbling block and participating in the demonic is just as surely God's Word to us today.

There are some guidelines that should help in determining what is culturally relative and what is transculturally permanent in the Bible. First, one should determine what is the central core of the message of the Bible and distinguish between the central core and what is on the fringe of the Bible. The holy kiss and women's head coverings are surely not at the central core of the Bible's concern.

Secondly, one should note whether the matter in hand is basically moral or nonmoral. For most Evangelicals, it would appear that eating food offered to idols, a head covering for women when they pray or prophesy, women teaching in the church, and Paul's preference for not getting married are examples of issues not basically moral issues. Of course, they may become moral issues by their use or abuse in given contexts. On the other hand, adultery, idolatry, thievery, and greed are always wrong.

Thirdly, one should be able to distinguish between a principle and a specific application. Thus in 1 Corinthians 11:2-16, the principle seems to be that one should do nothing to distract from the glory of God (especially by breaking social customs) when the community is at worship. The specific problem of women wearing a veil seems to be relative since Paul appeals to "custom" or "nature." Omission of a veil does not appear to distract in the twentieth century.

Fourthly, one must keep alert to possible cultural differences between the first and twentieth centuries that are not immediately obvious. For example, to determine the role of women in the twentieth-century church, one should take into account that there were few educational opportunities for women in the first century. In contrast, such education is generally expected in modern Western society. This may affect our understanding of such texts as 1 Timothy 2:9-15.

Finally, one must exercise Christian love. Christians need to recognize the difficulties and open the lines of communication with one another. One can start by trying to define some principles, and by having love for and a willingness to be open toward those with whom one differs.

### Application of the Practical Principle

Women's place in worship, marriage, and the church should be an excellent subject for discussion of the way in which the Bible is to be interpreted.

1. A text must be treated within its full unit of meaning. The reference to wives being subject to their husbands (Eph. 5:22-24) can be adequately understood only in terms of the mutual subjection commanded in verse 21, the sacrificial love of the husband prescribed in verses 25-30, and the unity of the marriage partners (v. 31-33).

2. The historical context of a passage helps the interpreter understand both the function and the meaning a text had in its own day. Did the actions and words of Jesus and Paul function to reinforce first-century beliefs in regard to women, or were they liberating even in their own day? When we consider the evident inferior status of women in biblical times, the meaning of the New Testament's advice to women changes drastically. We must ask whether we are not being unfaithful to the biblical message if we use Scripture's liberating words concerning women to impede the leavening process the words were meant to have.

For example, the meaning of 1 Timothy 2:8-15, which places various restrictions on women's dress and speech, was not given in our twentieth-century context. In contrast, the context was the double background of Paul's Judaism (where women were excluded from learning) and the situation at Ephesus (where untrained women who had submitted to heretical teachers seem to have been seeking to spread their beliefs, perhaps like the prostitutes in the service of the temple of Diana, compare 2 Tim. 3:5-7). Rabbinic law and Greek custom, as well as the particular situations being addressed, add necessary background and coloring to a correct twentieth-century understanding and application of the 1 Timothy text. It is also probable that, since women are found teaching (Acts 18:26) and prophesying (Acts 21:8; 1 Cor. 11:5) elsewhere in the New Testament, 1 Timothy 2:11-12 speaks to a local problem.

3. The biblical author's openly stated intention, methodology, theology, and practice as understood in other biblical texts which he has written can provide helpful clues for proper interpretation. Paul's specific advice concerning women in the church and family can be better understood if it is viewed as part of his larger intention to bring order to the Christian community. It is clear from his discussion of slavery in Philemon that Paul's method for social change was characterized by caution and orderliness.

Perhaps Paul's theological statement of equality of sexes in Christ found in Galatians 3:28 can help the interpreter understand the particularity and cultural-directedness of other parts of his advice (for example, 1 Cor. 14:34-35). Finally, the extensive description of Paul's ministry which is found in Acts, as well as the mention of current church practice within his Epistles, shows Paul's attitude toward women through his action (compare Acts 16:13; 17:4; Titus 2:3; 1 Cor. 11:5; Rom. 16:1-16). Phoebe was a deaconess in Cenchrea. Priscilla was Paul's fellow worker.

4. The Bible has an overarching consistency despite its varied theological emphases. Thus, all interpretations of given texts should be correlated with wider biblical attitudes, statements, themes, and descriptions. If husbands are to duplicate Jesus' attitude toward leadership, they might consider Matthew 20:25-28. Is it not true that the church as the body of Christ is ordered according to gift rather than gender (1 Cor. 12:4-7,12-25; Eph. 4:7-13; Rom. 12:6-8)? Finally, the Gospels describe women as being significantly involved in declaring the faith (John 4:39; 20:15-18; Matt. 28:9-10).

5. Insight into texts which are obscure must be gained from those which are plain. Here is a key principle for the interpretation of women's place in the church. Ordinarily, interpretation procedure would suggest that Christians seeking guidance on this topic should first turn to the three passages which speak directly about this area (1 Tim. 2; 1 Cor. 11; 14). But all of these texts are extremely difficult to interpret; crucial words remain obscure and the addressed situations are difficult to reconstruct. In fact, the surface meaning seems to contradict other Pauline material and the methods of argument reflect cultural thought forms no longer in use. Given these difficulties in interpretation in the texts that seem most appropriate, the plain descriptions of the interaction of Jesus and Paul with women and the readily interpreted accounts of women's creation in Genesis take on increased significance.

6. Scripture should be read with the centrality of Christ in mind. The goal of Scripture is to help its reader "put on the Lord Jesus Christ" (Rom. 13:14; see Eph. 4:13). Any teaching regarding women must, therefore, square with the truth of the gospel and the world's hope "in Christ." Christ's victory over sin and death has brought with it new possibilities for redeemed humanity. Galatians 3:28 cannot be used as grounds for dismissing other texts, but neither can it be ignored as the ideal. Redeemed humanity in the church and Christian marriage should mirror creation's new order in Christ.

7. Interpreters of Scripture should seek the help of the Christian community, past and present, in order that insights can be shared, humility fostered, and biases of culture and theological tradition overcome. The Christian community can be wrong in its interpretation of Scripture, as the church's former position on slavery indicates. Only the church—past, present, and future—can correct narrow or private perspectives and cultural bias.

8. Scriptural interpretation must allow for continuing and new understanding as necessary implications are drawn out. What is being claimed here is the fact of progressive understanding, not of ongoing revelation. Obvious examples of this need which have surfaced previously are the church's doctrine of the Trinity and the Christian movement against slavery. Both are rooted in the biblical text, although both go beyond the Bible in their exact formulations. These new understandings of the meaning of the Bible are necessary implications which theological controversy and the new cultural situations have brought to light. The changing role of women in the church and family would seem to be another example of this principle.

Those opposed to change claim that modern culture has determined the church's interpretation of the biblical text. Although this is true in some cases, it need not follow that a person will do this just because he takes his context seriously. Instead of determining its interpretation, culture can serve the church by being the occasion for renewed reflection and debate. A progressive understanding of Scripture should be continual as situations alter, allowing new implications of the text to come to light.[3]

Contemporary Christian leaders are contrasting the study of the biblical materials about homosexuality and the somewhat similar situations related to slavery and feminism. Long-cherished positions of biblical interpretation regarding slavery and feminism have been changed by many Evangelicals. In the case of slavery and women's rights, there is considerable biblical data and the examples of Jesus and Paul to assist in this change (for example, Gal. 3:28; Gen. 1:27). But no one is seriously claiming among Evangelicals that Scripture in any way explicitly supports a homosexual union. In nonevangelical circles, Ruth and Naomi, and David and Jonathan are sometimes mentioned as possible biblical models of homosexual tendencies. It is also argued that the New Testament is against abuse and that private monogamous homosexuality between consenting adults is different. However, the lack of textual support for such claims has kept Evangelicals from using these models. The homosexuality Paul had in mind in Romans 1:24-28 is the homosexuality of choice between men and women similar to that of today. There remains the fundamental fact that there is no positive scriptural support for even a qualified homosexuality.

For Evangelicals, the biblical teaching against homosexuality seems strong. This teaching is bound up with the biblical doctrine of the human, rooted in the order of creation and spelled out by the law. It is reinforced by Paul's treatment of both the law (1 Tim. 1:9-11) and the kingdom of God (1 Cor. 6:9-11). Evangelicals should receive the corrections gay advocates can offer concerning mistaken or overstated statements, while continuing to assert in love that the traditional position concerning the sinfulness of all homosexual activity is true to the biblical teaching.[4]

### Fifth, the Importance of the Doctrine of Accommodation in Interpreting Scripture and Formulating Doctrine

God himself, according to John Calvin, stooped down to people by using human modes of thought and speech in order to be understood by mortals. Although the revelation of God in these historical forms prevents us from knowing God totally, they do not falsify or misrepresent God in any way.

It is quite unfortunate that the doctrine of accommodation has lost the prominent place it once held in Christian thought. Accommodation refers to the process by which God adjusts to human capacities what he wills to reveal of the infinite mysteries of his being. Obviously, these mysteries are beyond the powers of the human mind to completely grasp.

Calvin always recognized that man is a creation and essentially remains a finite creature. In addition, man is by the sin of Adam and by his own rebellion a sinful creature. Thus, there is the necessity of the general accommodation of the infinite mysteries of God to finite comprehension, which embraces all revelation. There is also the necessity of the special, gracious accommodation to human sinfulness which is connected with the work of redemption.

In stooping down to our finite and sinful state, Calvin said, "God accommodates himself to the ordinary way of speaking on account of our ignorance, and sometimes, if I may be allowed the expression, stammers."

Revelation 19 describes Christ in his second coming as a rider on a white horse, with garments stained with blood. The instrument of Christ's conquest is to be the sharp sword that issues from his mouth (vv. 11-16). It is hardly possible to accurately equate this sword used by the conquering Christ with the weapons used by Charlemagne and Rome.

The military figures of speech are metaphors describing the glorious power which Christ the King shall exercise. However, this does not empty his coming and reign to the world of spiritual, nonspatial reality. But the weapons of his warfare may not be those of the earth. God's kingdom, whose instrumental King is Christ, operates by heavenly supernatural power. By such power, the kingdom was revealed in the person and earthly ministry of Christ. By such heavenly power, it is now proclaimed. And by the same power the kingdom shall be revealed at the time of his return.

Accommodation, with respect to all knowledge of God, was one of Calvin's basic methods and is helpful to us. In Calvin's view, man does not choose the symbols for the great unknown as is sometimes implied when the word "symbol" is used. Rather, knowledge about God begins and ends with the self-revelation of God. In his commentary on Isaiah 6:1, Calvin affirmed that the robe, throne, and bodily appearance of God are forms of revelation accommodated to human incapacities. However, said Calvin, "Lest we should suppose that the prophet Isaiah contrived the manner in which he would paint God, we ought to know that Isaiah faithfully describes the very form in which God was represented and exhibited to him."

The doctrine of accommodation, therefore, clearly points to the reality behind the symbols. Although the symbols, in some measure, distort that reality, they do so only in order to bring it within the reach of finite and sinful humanity. Calvin affirmed that there is no need for reality to agree at all points with a symbol if only the symbol suits sufficiently for the purpose at hand.

Actually, the fact that God chose to give his Word in ordinary human language, through real people, in real historical settings, is a part of the glory of the Bible. It is also a part of the glory of the Bible that God chose to speak his Word through a wide range of literary forms (narrative histories, chronicles, law codes, dramas, all kinds of poems, proverbs, prophetic oracles, parables, stories, letters, Gospels, and apocalypses). Each of these requires its own special rules for interpretation.

There is also a wide range of people who were used by the Holy Spirit to write Scripture. Thus we can distinguish between the way Paul and John expressed themselves theologically, as well as between their grammar and literary style. To say that they differed in expression is not to say that they were opposed or that one of them was in error.

Such expressions of accommodation are accepted by all Evangelicals. The real problem is, where do we draw the line? Do we start with a set idea in our mind and say what God *must* do, or do we start with the biblical text itself and say what God *did* do? Most Evangelicals prefer the latter option.

Take, for example, the question of whether accommodation allows for the human author to speak in popular language, even if such speech is not precise according to modern scientific norms. The Evangelical sees Jesus speaking popularly in Matthew 13:32 when he said that the mustard seed "is the smallest of all your seeds" (NIV). But if one argues that every botanical reference in Scripture must carry the precision of the twentieth-century botanist, then he must account for the fact that there are smaller seeds which have been discovered in other areas of the world. Was technical precision the purpose of Jesus or was he using a commonly held idea in his culture to illustrate the point of his parable?

John Jefferson Davis suggests that in the twentieth century something similar to Calvin's doctrine of accommodation can be used to deal with the problem of interpreting the early passages in Genesis. I have already noted that John in the Book of Revelation told of the distant future through images of his time. But there is reality behind the images he used. In the same manner, Davis suggests that the primeval past in Genesis is seen by the author of Genesis from the viewpoint of the second millennium BC.

A significant number of conservative writers during recent centuries have seen no conflict between a high doctrine of Scripture and the recognition of symbolic elements in the early chapters of Genesis. In Albertus Pieter's view, for example, the temptation and fall are actual historical events but are represented in symbolic form. J. I. Packer has admitted the difficulty of drawing hard and fast boundaries between the literal and the symbolic in the early chapters of Genesis. The conservative Old Testament scholar R. K. Harrison has suggested that the concept of "religious drama" might be an appropriate category for the narratives of the creation and fall.[5]

Davis suggests that it is important to avoid a "purely literal" versus "purely symbolic" conflict in relation to the historicity of the early chapters of Genesis in general and Genesis 3 through 4 in particular. This conflict can be avoided by utilizing terms developed by modern philosophy of language. The early Genesis narratives portray or picture historical realities after the fashion of an *analogue* or analogy. The acceptance of an *analogue* model is in keeping with the circumstance that the reality in question (the details of the Garden of Eden) is quite removed from the range of our normal experience. Descriptions of the end of history (the Book of Revelation) and the beginnings of history (early Genesis) all go beyond our normal experience, and our normal time and space categories must be stretched whenever we attempt to represent such realities.

In this view, features of the Genesis account, such as the trees in the Garden, the serpent, and the time framework (civilization was highly developed already in the second generation), are understood as modeling historical events but not in the sense of photographic identity. The interpretation of Genesis 3 and 4 proposed by Davis takes the text neither as a myth nor as a literal photographic likeness of the historical events. In contrast to the view that the fall is a myth, the features of the model proposed have a real connection with the particular events of actual, space-time reality. In contrast to strictly literal views, the features of the model are not understood in terms of a simple photographic likeness. The model describes, through figurative means, the actual flow of human history from the beginning.

Some tentative conclusions concerning the interpretation of Genesis 3 and 4 in terms of a redemptive-historical model can be suggested.

1. The narratives concern the actual, historical parents of the human race who were tempted by Satan, and who, through their fall, plunged the entire race into sin and death.

2. Features of the narrative, such as the trees in the Garden and the serpent, may be visual representations of invisible, spiritual realities.

3. In Genesis 3 and 4, there is a "telescoping" of the time span from the first generation to the development of civilization.

4. The cultural level implied by Genesis 4 is at least Neolithic and, in fact, represents the general cultural experience of the second millennium BC through whose categories the primeval history is presented.

5. The Adam of Genesis represents the first human being, both theologically and in terms of anthropology (the science and history of man).

6. Consequently, the conceptions of human origins as presented by Genesis and by anthropology, when both are properly understood, are not in contradiction but form a complementary whole.[6]

The proposal by Davis for interpreting the early Genesis account in terms of a redemptive-historical model is really an extension of the conservative principle of interpreting the text in the natural and intended sense. The Bible gives accurate and truthful information about science and history in a form appropriate to its own purposes. Those who hold to the complete trustworthiness of Scripture have nothing to fear from honest scientific and historical research, for the God of nature and history is also the God of the Bible.

We should also note that the fact of the reality of the historical existence of the first man and the fall will have important implications for the doctrines of man and salvation.

## Conclusion

By this time, it should be obvious that the matter of the method of properly interpreting the Bible is crucial. Our basic source of doctrine is the written Word of God. The task of this chapter has been to outline a method of freeing that Word to speak to our situation. Many of the issues of disagreement, such as the question of women's ministries in the church and the meaning of the early chapters of Genesis, are related to matters of biblical interpretation and not to a lack of commitment to the totally trustworthy Bible. They are questions of interpretation and have to do with our historical distance from the text and the question of the differences in culture. We will not all agree on the principles I have suggested. But surely we must agree that the question of the proper methods of interpretation is the arena in which we must carry on the discussion and not just in the arena of belief in the trustworthiness of the Bible.

The principles of interpretation which have been outlined should be seen as more than rigid and mechanical rules. They are helpful guidelines for Christians as we seek to improve our biblical understanding and to accept the resources and guidance which God has given to us in and through the Bible. Improper habits of biblical interpretation should be admitted and rejected. Constant practice and dialogue with other inter- preters should be encouraged. Since dozens of radical cults today claim to get their teachings from the Bible, it is imperative that we understand and put into practice these generally accepted principles of interpreta- tion.

In Ephesians 4:14, Paul stated that Christians should not be tossed to and fro and carried about with every wind of doctrine, by the cunning of men or by their craftiness in deceitful wiles. In this passage, Paul used metaphors from sailing and gambling that could be applied to biblical interpretation. The ship of biblical interpretation is tossed back and forth in the winds of new ideas. Gospel gamblers throw the dice of questionable interpretation about in cunning and crafty ways that deceive immature individuals.

We need to grow in our understanding of the Bible. But in Ephesians 4:15, Paul said that this growth needs to be accompanied by love. It is not enough to speak the truth that people should grow in knowledge. Paul added that truth needs to be spoken in love. Lack of love may create stubborn resistance even to that which people know to be truth. It takes more than truth to transform the heart. In the words of Paul, "Rather, speaking the truth in love, we are to grow up in every way into him who is the head, into Christ" (Eph. 4:15).

### Notes

1. John Bright, *The Authority of the Old Testament* (Nashville: Abingdon Press, 1967), p. 215-216.

2. A. Berkeley Mickelsen, *Interpreting the Bible* (Grand Rapids, MI: Eerdmans, 1963), p. 319.

3. Robert K. Johnston, *Evangelicals at an Impasse* (Atlanta: John Knox Press, 1979), pp. 69-75.

4. Ibid., pp. 143-145.

5. Roger R. Nicole and J. Ramsey Michaels, eds., *Inerrancy and Common Sense* (Grand Rapids, MI: Baker Book House, 1980), pp. 152-154.

6. Ibid., pp. 158-159.

### Bibliography

Davis, John Jefferson, ed. *The Necessity of Systematic* Theology, 2nd ed. Grand Rapids, MI: Baker Book House, 1978.

Fee, Gordon D., and Stuart, Douglas. *How to Read the Bible for All It's Worth.* Grand Rapids, MI: Zondervan, 1982.

Newport, John P. *Why Christians Fight Over the Bible.* Nashville: Thomas Nelson Inc., 1974.

Sire, James W. *Scripture Twisting.* Downer Grove, IL: InterVarsity Press, 1980.

Sproul, R.C. *Knowing Scripture.* Downers Grove, IL: InterVarsity Press, 1977.

Wells, William W. *Welcome to the Family: An Introduction to Evangelical Christianity.* Downers Grove, IL: InterVarsity Press, 1979.

# 6
## God, Creation, the Fall, Common Grace, and Providence

### The Person of God

The skyscraper is to be erected. We watch the foundation area being excavated. The blueprints are completed. The materials are available. Next, the framework of the building rises from the ground. There is a likeness between building a skyscraper and constructing a system of Christian doctrine. Most books on Christian doctrine follow a basic skeleton or framework, although there are some differences in arrangement and emphases. We will now project and fill out our framework. Our resources are the Bible and the history of doctrine using our guiding key and guiding method.

#### God Is Assumed

In our structure, the doctrine of God is usually placed first because Christian doctrine is primarily a reflection on God and his acts and revelation in history. The doctrine of God could be placed last since the character of God takes form in and through his redemptive activity in history.

The Bible, and thus Christian doctrine, does not begin with an attempt to prove the existence of God. Rather, the Bible assumes that God is. This is similar to the scientist who assumes the orderliness of the universe. The Christian theologian assumes a personal God who gives to life unity, wholeness, and hope and who has revealed himself progressively in redemptive history from Abraham to Jesus Christ and the apostles.

#### God's Self-Disclosure

The biblical teaching on revelation insists that God discloses or uncovers himself by his initiative, without which there would be no saving knowledge of God. A simple analogy of God's revelation is the revelation of one person to other persons. Human beings can only be known by others if they choose to reveal who they are to other people. Even the sciences which deal with understanding humanness depend upon human self-disclosure for their knowledge. This fact is particularly self-evident in intensive psychotherapy or psychoanalysis. Since the human psyche is to be healed, the psychotherapist is dependent upon the self-revelation of the patient. Without that, he is helpless. Unless the patient intentionally or unintentionally reveals himself, the therapist cannot treat the psychic sickness.

As the human person is known only through his self-revelation, so is God to be known. If one is serious about knowing God, one must turn to the Bible. It is the result of the revelation of God in a series of self-disclosures in a continuous history, first to Israel and then to the new Israel, the church. In one sense, what the Bible says God *is* really amounts to saying what he *does.* The terms of the description of his nature are really terms of his function and behavior. Therefore, the attributes or qualities ascribed to God are primarily descriptions of his acts.

The Bible insists not only that God's dealings with Israel and the church, as recorded in the Bible, reveal his will and ways in a uniquely significant manner but also that certain events within that history are uniquely significant as revelation. In Jewish faith, this crucial event is the *event at Sinai,* understanding by this phrase the whole complex of events that begins with the call of Moses and ends in the reception of the Torah (Law). Exodus-Sinai was for Israel the interpretive center of redemptive history, as the incarnation, the cross, and the resurrection are for the Christian. Other visitations of God, before and after, yield their deepest meaning when seen with eyes of faith from the perspective of these events of Sinai and Jesus Christ.

### God Is Revealed as Personal

The Bible reveals a personal God who is the source, maintainer, and goal of everything. This means that God is not a mere impersonal force or energy or existent substance. God is person. God has personality. Personality requires two basic characteristics. One is self-reflection, which means that he is self-conscious. The other is self-determination which means that he thinks and acts.

The biblical view stands opposed to pantheism (god is all) which depersonalizes God. Pantheism identifies god with everything—good, bad, and indifferent. In pantheism, there is no final distinction between god and the world. God minus the universe equals nothing.

Classical Hindu thought tends to be pantheistic. This type of Hinduism states that to think of God as a person is to set limits to him. Hindus say nothing positive about God. The divine in you is identical with Brahman (god). The separate existence of God or man is illusion or semi-illusion.

The Buddhists say that ultimate reality is Nirvana (there is nothing which has separate existence). God and man are emptied of separate personality. In contrast, the Christian seeks to be emptied so he can be filled with the fullness of the personal God revealed in Jesus Christ.

The God of Christian doctrine is a personal agent who acts. Creation is not a natural event with natural causes. Creation along with the incarnation of Jesus, the prophetic word, and the church were intentional acts of a personal God. Miracles in the New Testament are signs of God's activity which make us marvel at his power and purpose.

One implication of the personality of God is that we are like him. Humans are persons and free agents. We are able to go beyond, in some ways, the cause-and-effect processes that normally rule. In this regard, we are made in God's image. But God has no roots in nature, and he is absolutely free while we are finite (less than God and limited). God is not less than our own self-directive, purposive, free-choosing selves. He is inexhaustibly more so. God is, in fact, the only self-existent being.

#### God Is Revealed as One

The Christian view of God is opposed to polytheism (many gods). Polytheism was widespread in the ancient Near East. But the Old Testament faith, out of which Christianity came, emphasized the oneness of God. So God is the one prime existent, the one prime reality, and the one source of all reality.

#### God Is Revealed as Three-in-One

The importance of the three-in-oneness of God is seen in the central place this belief commands in Christian worship. Many of our services include a doxology, such as: "Praise God from whom all blessings flow;

Praise him, all creatures here below; Praise him above, ye heav'nly host; Praise Father, Son, and Holy Ghost."

Another well-known hymn begins with the verse: "Holy, holy, holy! Lord God Almighty! Early in the morning our song shall rise to thee; Holy, holy, holy, merciful and mighty! God in three Persons, blessed Trinity!"

In the majority of Christian traditions, Christians are baptized in the name of the Father and the Son and the Holy Spirit. Usually we are married in the same threefold Name.

*Two heresies regarding the Trinity.*—Unfortunately, many Christians deviate from a proper understanding of the Trinity. Some are virtually "tritheists." This means that the Father, the Son, and the Holy Spirit are regarded practically as three separate gods. Other professing Christians are almost Unitarians. Both of these approaches are serious deviations from orthodox Christianity. The first amounts to a form of Christian polytheism. The group that is close to Unitarianism has really fallen back into Judaism or a kind of Christian Islam. This view holds that the Father is God and Jesus is his prophet, while the Holy Spirit is almost completely left out.

*The centrality of the Trinity in early Christian experience.*—The tendency to heresy requires us to seek the proper understanding of the Trinity from the Bible and Christian history. An implication of the personality of God, as taught in the Bible, is that God is not simple unity but a unity of complexity. The Bible reveals God as not only personal and one but also as Triune (three-in-one). This means that within the one essence of the godhead we have to distinguish three persons. These three persons are neither three gods nor three parts or modes of God. Rather, these three persons are coequally and coeternally God.

It should be noted that there is no detailed doctrine of the Trinity in the Bible. But the understanding of the early Christians of the person of Christ and the salvation provided by him and the Holy Spirit became the framework for the earliest statements of the tri-unity of God. This idea of the Trinity was built up from the threefold activity of God in history as Creator and Sustainer, as Redeemer and Reconciler, and as Re-creator and Sanctifier. God is known in three mighty acts: creation, incarnation, and the outpouring of the Holy Spirit. These three acts were seen as the Father, Son, and Spirit in their respective missions. Jesus Christ is an objective revelation of God in history. The Holy Spirit carries forward the historical redemptive work of Christ and makes it real in our lives.

Thus we see that the doctrine of the Trinity was central in early Christian experience. The coming of Jesus and the Holy Spirit set in motion the transformation of Jewish monotheism into the Christian doctrine of the Trinity (2 Cor. 13:14).

*Foregleams of the Trinity in the Old Testament.*—Although the main evidence for the doctrine of the Trinity is to be found in the New Testament, we need to begin with the Old. No statement of belief is complete unless it is set within the context of the whole Bible.

Obviously, on first approach, the Old Testament has a main emphasis on the unity of God. God is all on his own. He has no relations. The first of the Ten Commandments, which is basic to all the other Commandments, is: "You shall have no other gods before me" (Ex. 20:3).

Although there is this strong emphasis upon the oneness of God, a group of ideas in the Old Testament play a part in the reflection of the New Testament writers. These concepts are the word of God, the wisdom of God, and the Spirit of God (Isa. 55:11; Prov. 8; Gen. 1:2).

Although the Old Testament writers believed that God is the transcendent One, over and above humanity, they also believed that he actively intervenes in the world. They indicated that God is personal and personally active. This is particularly true of the word of God, the wisdom of God, and the Spirit of God. These are three very powerful extensions of his personality. There is movement in the living God. His being is not rigid and motionless but constantly reaches out toward others.

Both Paul and John took up the idea of the word and wisdom of God and applied it to Jesus Christ (John 1:1-2; 1 Cor. 1:24). The idea of the Spirit of God develops into a purely personal understanding of Spirit, which is known as the Holy Spirit (John 16:13-14).

So the Old Testament provides ground for the growth of belief in God as Trinity which was more openly expressed in the New Testament. The doctrine was to develop along mainly Greek lines, but the basis for it was already in Jewish thought.

*The Trinity in the New Testament.*—In the New Testament, the Father and Jesus are clearly distinguished. Yet the same writers said, with equal emphasis, that Jesus Christ is also God. Jesus was worshiped. Quotations from the Old Testament were transferred from the Lord God to Christ.

Jesus performed the divine functions of creation, forgiveness, and judgment.

Several biblical authors stated that Jesus was preexistent and came from the Father. Paul summarized it when he wrote that "in him [Jesus Christ] the whole fulness of deity dwells bodily" (Col. 2:9; see John 1:1).

In the Gospels, we read comparatively little about the Spirit. But John wrote, "As yet the Spirit had not been given, because Jesus was not yet glorified" (John 7:39). After Pentecost the image of the Holy Spirit becomes much clearer. He was seen as much more than a divine power. He is a divine person. Again and again, personal names and activities were ascribed to him. He led, allowed, and was made sad. Only one conclusion is possible:—the Spirit of God himself is with and in believers.

We summarize the New Testament picture of God by saying that God is one. But on the other hand, this one God exists as Father, Son, and Holy Spirit. This threefold nature of God is present throughout the whole New Testament. It is a pattern to be seen everywhere (2 Cor. 13:14). It is true that the New Testament teaching does not constitute a full doctrine of the Trinity, but it lays a foundation for such a doctrine. There is enough proof in the New Testament that the later doctrine of the Trinity, as formulated by the church in its creeds, is not a foreign element imposed upon the New Testament. Rather, the Trinity is a natural consequence of the New Testament witness.

After much discussion in the first three centuries of Christian history, the early church fathers largely agreed that God not only reveals himself as Father, Son, and Holy Spirit but also *is* Father, Son, and Holy Spirit. These three names indicate three genuine distinctions within the one personal God. These three distinctions themselves are fully personal.

The Trinity is certainly a great mystery. What is important is to note that the Trinity confirms the communal and personal nature of God. The Trinity means that God is himself a blessed community of love. God is not only an actually existent being but is personal; persons can relate to him in a personal way, as we do to our own fathers. God reveals himself as a single God who is a fellowship of love among three "persons."

And this is not just theory for Christian believers. We know by experience that we are children of the Father, that we are redeemed by the Son, and that the Holy Spirit is in our lives. And Christians also know that in all three relationships we have the one and same God.

We experience the threefoldness of the Father, Son, and Holy Spirit in our lives. And yet there is the experience of unity, too, especially as the Spirit dwells in us. In and through the Spirit, Jesus Christ himself is present with us; in and through Jesus, we have fellowship with God the Father.

## Qualities of God

When we follow the acts of God and read the interpretation of their meaning by the inspired prophets and apostles, certain qualities or characteristics of God emerge. Theologians usually call these the formal and material qualities of God.

### The Formal Qualities of God

*Transcendent.*—The God who acts in our history is not one being among other beings. God is not just a superperson complete with body parts. He transcends (goes beyond) space and time. He is Spirit. He stands over against the world even while being a full participant in its history (John 4:24; Col. 1:15; 1 Tim. 1:17). The idea that God is beyond us and our world is sometimes difficult to understand. Look at a stone: God is not it; God is beyond it. Look at people: God is not us; God is beyond us. Yet God is not so beyond that he bears no relation to us and our world.

God is unlimited and beyond us in terms of time. His realm is eternity. Our very notion of time is bound up with the movement of the stars and planets which he created. But God is not bound by this system.

The fact that God is above time certainly does not mean that God is merely static. The God of the Bible stands in active relationship with the universe which he created. We are creatures in time and so if God is to reveal himself to us it must be in terms of history, of sequence, of before and after. Jesus lived and died and rose again, the perfect manifestation of God within time, at a specific place in history.

*Immanent.*—The Bible is unintelligible apart from the assumption of the presence of the purposing God in nature, persons, historical happenings and structures, and especially in the Person and work of Jesus Christ. *Immanence* (with us) is the abstract word for this involvement in our world. It means God is holding the world together, working creatively, resisting destructive powers, and working in Israel, Jesus Christ, the church and the larger world.

Look at a stone: God is present. Look at people: God is present. Is this, then, a contradiction to the teaching that God is beyond us? Is Christian doctrine nonsense at this point? I think not.

God is unlimited in place. He is everywhere. Theologians call this *omnipresence.* It is impossible to hide from God or to escape from him. He is everywhere. But it does not follow that he cannot sometimes appear to people in a localized way. He appeared in the Old Testament to his people in a particular place in a bright cloud of glory, at the tent in the wilderness, and at the Temple.

In the New Testament, God met his people in the most humanly personal way possible, through his Son Jesus. When Jesus was in Galilee, he was not in Jerusalem or Jericho; he was spatially restricted. But God himself was not thereby restricted to any one location, for Jesus continued to pray to him as his "Father in heaven."

In other words, just as God is timeless but meets us in history, so is he omnipresent but meets us in his Son Jesus. And Jesus lived in a real place, Palestine, and met his people in separate encounters on known roads, in boats, and in houses. Today he meets with us by his Holy Spirit.

A well-known Christian writer illustrates the transcendence and immanence of God by telling of an experience related to his five-year-old daughter named Carol and her mother. Carol and her mother were in the kitchen, and her mother was teaching her about God's being everywhere. So Carol asked, "Is God in the living room?" "Yes," her mother replied. "Is he in the kitchen?" "Yes," she said. "Am I stepping on God?"

Suddenly the mother was speechless. But look at the point that was raised. Is God here in the same way a stone or a chair or a kitchen is here? No, not quite. God is immanent, here, everywhere, in a sense completely in line with his transcendence. For God is not matter as you and I, but Spirit. And yet he *is* here. Jesus Christ is said to be "upholding the universe by his word of power" (Heb. 1:3). That is, God is beyond all, yet in all and sustaining all.[1]

*God as immutable.*—In God's actions we see his steadfastness or unchanging purpose (Ps. 102:27; Jas. 1:17). God is immutable (does not change). His life does not change, his character does not change, and his ways do not change. Furthermore, his purposes do not change. Even his Son does not change. For this reason, God is supremely reliable and trustworthy.

It is important to understand this changelessness of God correctly. It does not mean that he is passionless or that he cannot feel a variety of emotions. The Bible shows us the God who feels very deeply (Hos. 11:8). It furthermore does not mean that his dealings with a particular person or nation may not change in their experience. Rather, it means God's dealings with us will always be based on what God is like.

*God as all-sufficient.*—The Bible points out that God is able to accomplish the divine purpose. This means that he is all-sufficient, as expressed in his all-sufficient presence, knowledge, and power. God alone is self-existing. This means that, whereas everything and everyone else depend on him for existence, he is absolutely independent of them. He has life in himself, and he is the source of the life of the universe. However, he himself has no source. He alone is utterly self-sufficient.

Closely related to God's all-sufficiency is the fact that God is unlimited in knowledge. He is omniscient. There is nothing that God does not know. He knows the future as well as the past and present. The author of Psalm 139 expressed beautifully his amazement at God's being everywhere, knowing him even as he was being formed in his mother's womb.

God is also unlimited in power. This is called the omnipotence of God. But this fact, frequently stressed in the Bible, is often applied wrongly. God cannot do anything that would violate his own character or break one of his promises. When Christians say that God is omnipotent, they simply mean that there is no limit to his power. He has no built-in or intrinsic weakness or inability. He can do anything he pleases. But what he pleases will always be in perfect harmony with his character and with all that makes him God.

### The Material Qualities of God

There are various ways of expressing these so-called material qualities of God, but the two defining characteristics or qualities are holiness and love. God is utterly righteous and holy in his glory and holds us accountable for our disobedience. And yet, as the Bible so clearly states, joined to this holiness and majesty is a long-suffering compassion.

*Holiness and love.*—Holiness emphasizes God's absolute righteousness which condones or approves no shadow of evil. As the apostle John wrote, "God is light and in him is no darkness at all" (1 John 1:5). God's holiness is his separateness from all that smacks of evil. But God's goodness is also expressed as love. In fact, John said, "God is love"

(1 John 4:16). This leads God to self-sacrifice and the full extension of his favor to man.

These two attributes of God most completely sum up all that he has revealed of himself. Holiness sums up the nature of God. The holy God is also the loving God. God's love is not caused by anything in the ones whom he loves but finds its springs in God's own character. His love is directed toward the lost world. His greatest demonstration came when he sent his Son to reconcile us to himself (John 3:16).

There is no authentic doctrine without the paradoxical (humanly contradictory) statement that God is both holy and love. Although we cannot explain this paradox, Christian believers experience the unity of holiness and love in their encounter with the Christian gospel. At the cross, God's harshest judgment took the form of total love. Also at the cross, we see the depth of our own sin which helped bring Christ to the cross. We also see in the cross the love that accepts and forgives the sinner. We then see that God's love has paid the price for us, absorbing the divine judgment.

*Holiness and love and the Christian life.*—Out of this experience the Christian way of life grows. Those who cannot live with the strain and pain of paradox relax the tension by eliminating one of the two elements of holiness and love. The more liberal Christians tend to dissolve the holiness and emphasize the love (for example, there is no hell and all people will be saved). The more orthodox Christians tend to overemphasize the holiness and judgment of God. However, authentic Christians must balance holiness and love. They realize that they have been shown compassion and so they are able to forgive and express compassion and mercy. Holy love is central, but this kind of love cannot violate its holy base. It cannot be transformed into sentimental indulgence and cheap grace. It must satisfy the demands of righteousness. That is why the profoundest levels of the divine life are those of suffering love, the pain of God in Christ which purges sin, conquers evil, and overcomes death.

Out of this vulnerability (openness), the Christian way of life grows. The believer has been shown compassion, and the forgiven sinner is able to forgive sinners. But this forgiveness is no more devoid of righteousness than is the model of holy love, a compassion and mercy joined to a passion for justice, a love of the sinner but wrathful with the sin.

The Christian life, short of the new heaven and the new earth, never achieves the perfection of the divine unity of holiness and love. But confessing that we miss the mark, we nevertheless seek to move toward the unity of holiness and love.

*Practical implications.*—The importance of both holiness and love can be seen in some of the developments in Christian circles today. For example, some Christian leaders fail to prophetically denounce those who live at the pinnacles of power and misuse power, a judgment found in both the Old and New Testaments. Fundamental truths about God's holiness are filtered out of the preaching of many Christian leaders.

### The Mystery and Response

As indicated, there is a necessary mystery related to God's nature. We can understand some of his qualities by analogy with human experience. We have seen that God is both loving toward sinners and angry with them. The closest analogy might be a good mother or father who both loves and is angry with a disobedient child.

But God is far beyond our limitations. This means that we need to admit that we do not know all about God's character. We can only know what God discloses of himself. To claim we know more about God than he has revealed is a mark not of knowledge but of arrogance.

In fact, worship is the finest response to the God who made us and who, despite our persistent rebellion and indifference, still delights to make himself known. Such a God will move us to profound adoration, to thinking about him on the large scale.

We must, therefore, refuse to speculate about God in a way different from his character that he has made known in the Bible. In fact, God has made himself known to us not primarily to satisfy our curiosity but to meet our needs. God reveals his compassion to us because we are lost and guilty. He reveals his eternity to us to keep us from being too preoccupied with this passing world scene and thus neglect the kingdom concerns and purposes.

## The Backdrop of God's Creation of the World

My son wanted to sell his house. A buyer was ready. But it was discovered that the house did not have a sound foundation. The buyer refused to consider the house until a stable and firm foundation was provided.

Apart from the doctrine of God, the doctrine of creation is the foundation stone of the whole edifice or building which we call Christian doctrine. It is a basic doctrine. Before other doctrines are considered, the doctrine of creation must be carefully stated and established.

### The Importance of the Doctrine of Creation

Early Christian theology used the biblical teaching on creation to reject the changeable moods and whims of the pagan gods (such as Zeus) as an explanation of the world's origin and development. Today, on the same basis, the Christian rejects ideas of origin which speak of chance, accident, spontaneous generation, or naturalistic evolution.

Creation stands first in the order of God's works. It marks both the beginning of all that is distinct from God and the beginning of time.

Creation is also crucial because the created world is the external setting for God's redemptive plan. The whole cosmos is the necessary stage for God's purpose. The creation of a unique covenant partner, man, with freedom to respond to God's invitation is also necessary. Creation also provides the context for human existence and man's relationship with God. Thus we see that creation makes God's redemptive covenant technically possible. It provides the spaces and furnishes the subjects.

### The Foreground of the Doctrine of Creation

In the Christian drama, there is no doubt that creation is the overflow of the reality of the inner depths of the nature of God. God did not have to create at all, let alone create the actual world he made. He created things for his own good pleasure and glory. But God did not will to be God without the world.

It has been suggested that creation is like human speech. Our speech implies intelligence and a desire to communicate. When we speak, it is not an accident nor a necessity. So it is with God's desire to create.

## God's Creation of the World

### Characteristics of the Created World

*God created the world out of nothing.*—God spoke the world into existence: "God said, 'Let there be light'; and there was light" (Gen. 1:3). Theologians thus say that God created the world out of nothing, not out of himself or some preexistent chaos. If the world were really preexistent, it would be as eternal as God.

*God created the world with meaning.*—Jesus Christ, the eternal Word, was the agent of creation (Col. 1:16). As the Word, Jesus Christ was not only personal but also the very designation of Christ as *Word* or *Logos* implies meaning (John 1:1). The created universe has meaning. Meaning is something that is built into the very structure of the universe by God as he created the world through Christ.

*God created the world as orderly.*—The prophet Isaiah, in 45:18-19, described the sense of order in creation. "For thus says the Lord,/who created the heavens/(he is God!),/who formed the earth and made it/(he established it;/he did not create it a chaos,/he formed it to be inhabited!):/'I am the Lord, and there is no other./I did not speak in secret,/in a land of darkness;/I did not say to the offspring of Jacob,/"Seek me in chaos."/I the Lord speak the truth,/I declare what is right.' "

God does not present us with confusion in creation but with clarity. There is an orderliness and a regularity to the universe. We can expect the earth to turn so the sun will rise every day.

Order in creation thus makes knowledge and science possible because it makes things intelligible, and we can learn how to act. Knowledge reveals our interdependence within an overall order (including the life-support systems) of which we are a part. A part of the wisdom that guides daily life comes from observing creation's order and taking heed.

The Bible teaches us to respect nature's order as God's gracious doing. The fear of the Lord is thus the beginning of wisdom (Ps. 111:10). This attitude was lacking in those Paul described in Romans 1, who served the creature rather than the Creator and exchanged the truth of God for a lie (v. 25).

Some theologians point out that there are different creation orders, such as those related to economics, politics, and family, which must be respected. Other theologians designate these creation orders as law spheres which point to the Creator. There are constants in every aspect of nature which have been created by God, and to know something about them is to know something about the will of God.

*God created the world as open.*—As we will see in the doctrines of continuing creation and providence, God is constantly involved in the unfolding pattern of his created universe. The universe was created as open, or not completely determined. As will be noted, humanity is also involved in this pattern, for good or bad.

If the universe were not orderly, our decisions would have no effect and we could not depend on their consequences. If the course of events were completely determined, our decisions would have no significance. So the Bible declares that the universe is orderly but not completely determined.

*God created the universe as good.*—The value judgment that the universe is good is given five times in Genesis 1. *Good* indicates that it was just what God planned. The creation in every part matched God's gracious purposes. This goodness is in marked contrast to the emphasis of the Greek philosopher, Plato, who saw the physical as less than real or good. Some of the Eastern and Western mystics also taught that nature is evil or only half real.

In the early centuries, some heretical teachers called Docetics taught that Jesus only appeared to have a physical body. They believed that Jesus could not have had a real physical body because of their belief that physical things were evil and Jesus was good. But the doctrine of creation teaches that evil is not inherent in the creation as such. Evil is not God's doing, nor were God's creatures originally made evil. Although a created being may stubbornly resist its purpose and refuse the ideal purpose of God, it is, in its most essential character, a good gift of God.

### God's Continuing Creation

The divine creativity is not limited to the beginning of the world for he is the living God, active in his creation. He did not stop being creative when he rested on the seventh day but remained actively involved.

The continuing existence of the world depends on the freedom of God to re-create and to perpetuate this great experience in covenant. The newness that marked the beginning continues. The process of creative transformation that has claimed the attention of contemporary science and philosophy is the continuing work of the God who "makes all things new" (Rev. 21:5).

This theme of continuing creation is found in many places in the Bible. Isaiah stated that: "The Lord is the everlasting God,/the Creator of the ends of the earth./He does not faint or grow weary,/his understanding is unsearchable./He gives power to the faint" (40:28-29). And Job, too, was reminded of the continued involvement of the Creator and of our dependence on the living God, the Lord of creation (chs. 38—41). The apostle Paul stated that in Christ the whole world holds together (Col. 1:17).

**Creation and the Trinity**

As was noted in the section on God, the work of creation is the labor of a Trinitarian God. Usually God the Father is seen in the forefront of creation. Yet the Son and the Spirit were and are present and active in creation. John 1:2-3 states that all things were made through the Word (Christ). The same partnership is true of the Holy Spirit who continues the creativity of the Father and the Son.

## God's Creation of Humanity

In an English private school, some of the students stated that the hope of civilization lay in the pursuit and application of scientific knowledge. They felt that religion had no place in an ideal society. Since this life is all, they thought they should enjoy it. When the principal of the school was asked for job and college references, he decided to phrase one of the references in a strictly scientific fashion. He wrote about one of the students in an impersonal, scientific manner. First, he said, "John is a mammal of the order *primate* and of the *sapiens* species. Chemically, John contains large quantities of carbon and various amounts of iron, calcium, magnesium, phosphorus, sulphur, lime, nitrogen, and some mineral salts. I hope John will fit in as an efficient unit into the various industrial and commercial organizations that make up our scientifically-planned society. Regrettably, however, I have serious misgivings about his conformity. He has a passionate love of music. He has confessed to a deep discontent because he cannot live up to his ideals. Thus it appears to me that John is on a quest that his human existence, even in a four-dimensional space-time continuum, can never satisfy."[2]

After reading the reference, John realized that such a scientific description left out much of what it means to be human. It is true that in some ways we are no different from animals. But the Bible says that people, created by God in his image, have unique dimensions not possessed by animals.

**Man as Created in the Image of God**

*Man is created for a special relationship to God.*—This relationship is a personal relationship because God is personal. Man is self-conscious and can make decisions. Furthermore, man can respond to God's claims.

*Man is created as a moral being with the knowledge of right and wrong.*

*Man is created as a rational and creative creature.*—We share in God's rationality (use of reason) which is seen in creation. Man's intelligence can be seen in the urge toward creativity—in art, science, religion, play. But this creativity has been infected by the blight and disease of sin.

*Man is created for fellowship with God.*—Man can only find true self-expression and deep fulfillment when he finds God.

*Man is created for eternal life with God.*—This eternal life is not ours by nature. It is God's gift in Jesus Christ which we either receive or reject.

*Man is created for dominion over the rest of creation.*—Man's higher position in creation is God-given. God is Lord of all, and in a limited fashion we share in his lordship. This characteristic involves man as steward. Stewards have no legal claims on the property, but they are in charge and answerable to the owner.

*Man is created for social relations.*—The first and most basic of all relationships is the unique pairing of husband and wife for the purpose of sharing, loving, and forming new life. In the Bible, sexuality is placed firmly within this setting. Sex is not a thing in itself, isolated from a continuing relationship. The creation account says, "It is not good that the man should be alone" (Gen. 2:18).

Christianity has sometimes encouraged a view of women as inferior to men before God and socially unequal in the community. Even some of the greatest church fathers were guilty of this.[3] In their eagerness to commend the advantages of chastity (no wife or sex relations) for Christian ministry, they accused women of wielding a sinful and seductive influence over men. Women have even been accused of causing humanity's fall.

Christians largely agree that God's nature lies beyond sexuality. God bears neither male nor female sexuality. However, in describing God, the Bible frequently uses both masculine images (father, shepherd, king) and feminine images (mother, hen). And so it affirms that both sexes have the task of reflecting the image of God.

This biblical emphasis rules out all sexist notions. There is no justification for male chauvinism or superiority. Women are not created as inferior creatures but as people of equal standing with men and equal dignity before God (Gen. 1:27). Here is a vital principle to grasp: women are spiritual beings endowed with exactly the same opportunities to find and know God as men are. The Bible never casts doubts about the worth of women, although it is true that it was not until the ministry of Jesus that the full teaching was reached about their spiritual nature and potential.

Within the marriage bond there are different roles for each partner to perform. This difference is obvious at one level: men cannot give birth nor nurse their young and women cannot give sperm. But at other levels, especially in our complex society, the roles are not as clear-cut as they used to be. Modern education and social pressure have given women a freedom undreamed of two decades ago. This is something to be deeply grateful for; yet, in its turn, it has an unhealthy side. The breakdown of marriages in industrial society is now a serious problem, and Christian insights into the nature of marriage are much needed (Eph. 5:21-33).

The Bible also points out that in the family, the different age generations are to be integrated on the basis of the honor that each has for the other. Although the New Testament lays a greater stress on the church as the center for fellowship, teaching, and service, it does teach that the relationship between parents and children is of fundamental importance (Eph. 6:1-4).

*Man is created as one human race.*—The central Christian view of race is that there is only one human race. The apostle Paul told the Athenians that God created every race of men of one stock to inhabit the whole earth's surface (Acts 17:26). At the pivotal points where God dealt with humanity, in creation and in re-creation in Christ, humankind is presented as indivisible in terms of race or color.

Race today is not thus understood. Groups of human beings are divided today into superficial "racial" categories: black, brown, white, red, mixtures. The Bible uses other categories: nation, culture, religion, and clan. This shows that the important differences are cultural, not biological.

*Man is created as finite.*—As creatures we live at the meeting point of nature and spirit. We were made finite beings by God. We are dependent on social and natural processes. Even our reason and spirit are shaped, although not completely determined, by physical and social factors. Our genes and our environment remind us of our derived existence (Ps. 90:3-12).

The implication of the unity of the spirit and the physical in humanity is that we are persons made up of body and spirit. Thus the privileges of the healthy and rich give them a freedom which is not enjoyed by the poor who are constricted by social and economic factors. We live at the meeting of nature and spirit and not in the realm of pure spirit. The Bible thus makes harsher judgments on the rich (Mark 10:21-24; Matt. 19:21-22; Luke 18:22-25; 1:53; 6:24; 16:19-31), and expects more from them (Luke 12:48). The inference would seem to be that the poor should be given the kinds of support which would undergird them as they seek to reach a certain dignity and proper moral and spiritual possibilities. This is not a hand-me-down emphasis but an undergirding and enabling emphasis. Just as in God's gift of salvation, we must respond and act.

## Creation and Science

### Claims and Problems of Evolution

Almost every layperson knows something of the dramatic story of the life and work of Charles Darwin. In 1859 he published *The Origin of the Species* which advanced the hypothesis of the organic evolution of all life.

For Darwin, life advanced and developed in terms of struggle for existence, survival of the fittest, heredity, variations, and natural selection. He affirmed that higher animals, including man, were evolved out of plants and they out of nonliving matter. The starting point was a primitive meaningless mass.

Since the publication of *The Origin of the Species,* extensive claims have been made for evolution. For some people, no other principle is needed to explain nature.

However, from the time that naturalistic evolution was advanced as a scientific hypothesis, many scientists have not been satisfied. For these scientists, the naturalistic evolutionary hypothesis could not account for the way in which small variations could remain until the time for a new species to develop. The problem of missing links between humans and the ape is a real issue.

Thus scientists tend to divide themselves into two groups. Many continue to believe that Darwin's view of natural selection offers the only key necessary to biological understanding. On the other hand, some deny that natural selection is inclusive or broad enough to account for all data.

Development in biology appears to proceed on the basis of law and not chance. It is difficult to assume that the arrangement for life on this planet is all by chance. Even our sensory organs appear to be geared to nature. Above all, naturalistic evolution cannot account for the unique nature of man.

The primary point of difference, then, between naturalistic evolution and some type of purposive developmental creationism is not a matter of accepting or rejecting facts. The primary point of difference is at the level of *mechanistic versus purposive* presuppositions. It is easy to see why the theory of naturalistic evolution has been and is upsetting to many Christian people. Darwinism, or at least secular versions of it, suggests that humans are not the apex or climax of God's creative process. Rather, humans are temporary products of random factors and casual sequences in the shifting realm of nature. The sources of human life come from a chance variation within the passage of countless generations. As the dinosaurs rose and passed away for no reason at all except the wind of chance and the laws of survival, so it will be with humankind. This view is obviously opposed to the view of evangelical Christians.

### The Bible and Science

In the forefront of problems connected with the theory of evolution is its relation to the Genesis account of creation. This fact is paradoxical (humanly contradictory) and ironic. The basic affirmations of Genesis provide some of the necessary foundations for the development of Western science of which Darwinism or evolution is certainly a result.

The biblical view states that creation is good. It likewise affirms that time moves forward in a line and does not reverse itself and, therefore, is capable of cumulative development. This is a very important background factor in the development of biological science. In this sense, the Genesis account has undergirded many of the fruitful concepts which have developed from the work of the biologists.

### The Purpose of Genesis and the Bible

But whatever its place as a background for science, the chief purpose of the Bible is redemptive or religious. The Bible is obviously given by God to help us interpret and evaluate the world of experience and find redemptive power and salvation.

Since this is the primary purpose of the Bible, it contains a quite limited amount of material dealing with nature. This fact suggests that no full technical story concerning nature is undertaken. The details of creation and natural science are not a major topic of the Scriptures except in terms of broad affirmations. God accommodated himself (spoke down) to man in communicating these truths about nature.

The Genesis account of the creation of nature and man is prescientific (not antiscientific). It is in outline form. The account is noted for its bold affirmations or statements that God is the unconditioned sole creator and that his creation is systematic and planned.

The main thrust of the Genesis account is that man is a special creation of a unique type. Evil is the result of the first man, and every person following him, rebelling against the Creator. We marvel that the biblical writers were so guided and inspired that they were enabled to see and understand in a clear way basic facts of life from the redemptive perspective. The contrast of the biblical accounts of creation with other nonbiblical statements is noteworthy and significant.

### The Christian and Evolution

What is to be a Christian's attitude toward naturalistic evolution? Christians have taken and do take many attitudes.

*Fiat Creationism.*—This is the theory that God instantaneously or in a short period of time spoke into existence all species and forms of mineral, vegetable, animal, and human life.

*Theistic Evolutionists.*—Under the impact of modern discovery, other Christians have become convinced that some form of evolution or development is a fact. For them evolution becomes simply the methodology used by God to bring to pass the forms of life.

This view emphasizes the immanence or indwelling power of God in nature. Instead of creating anew each species, God used what he had already completed as the basis for the next step in his creative plan. Such a well-known Christian theologian as A. H. Strong was sympathetic with theistic evolution.

Although some Evangelicals today hold to a form of theistic evolution, the majority hold to one of the theories involving creationism.

*Progressive Creationism or Dynamic Creationism.*—Progressive creationism can be characterized by three general affirmations. First, there were broad concepts in the mind of God. Following this, there were continuing acts of instantaneous creation by God, especially in terms of root species, which differentiates this view from theistic evolution. God also worked immanently or in an indwelling way in the process through the Holy Spirit. The so-called laws of nature were under the direction of the Holy Spirit actualizing over a long period of time and through process the plan of God. Thus we see that immediate creation *and* development or process are both important categories in this view.

In broad summary, many evangelical Christians contend that the reconciliation of science and religion is possible only in terms of the Christian faith. The modern scientific tradition already has its roots in the Christian tradition. It should be brought back into the Christian context out of which it sprang. Above all, in this atomic age, much depends on the purpose for which science is used. Christianity contends that it can provide both the creative and worthy purpose and the spiritual power and moral guidelines which are needed.

## Implications of the Doctrine of Creation

### Nature

Nature is not to be seen primarily as something to be used for man's selfish purposes. Rather, nature is to be seen and used from God's perspective. The implication is that technology must value all creation and that all life is essential to the ecosystem (life support system) that God has made. There should be the stewardship of natural resources, the proper care of animal life, and a sensitive ecological ethic that sees nature and human nature being mutually supportive. The cultivation of the fruit of creation does not call for their selfish exploitation. Human nature and nature are to be seen as partners in creation.

Technology must not dehumanize but, by just distribution, must contribute to the human quality of our earthly existence. God usually works through human creativity, science, and technology; people do change the course of history, and we can avert evils. We must, therefore, nourish responsible human creativity under God's guidance.

### Work

The purpose of work is to provide for the human needs of all people and for a truly human quality of life. Work is service: serving God, our fellowmen, and ourselves.

### Creativity

The character of God as seen in creation shows an overwhelming imagination. God's world is full of surprises, including humankind's ability to make new things. The variety of the ways God has expressed himself is boundless, which demonstrates how interested he is in material things. It is his character to express himself. The earth shows the work of his hands.

God commands men and women to make use of these created things and to explore and utilize creation. Humankind has a role in God's world as manager. This role requires imagination, sensitivity, and action. The purpose of culture is to make the world a better place and also to return to God with interest the gifts he has given to humanity.

Part of our calling and our creation mandate is art, celebration, recreation, and a good time. A free spirit requires freedom from thinking and acting as if life itself depends altogether on me. It is an attitude that carries over into all of life, finding expression in whatever we do.

It is not surprising that different theological emphases affect attitudes toward creativity. Traditions with a strong emphasis on the physical in creation, incarnation, and sacrament, like the Roman Catholic and Anglican, have generally been productive in the arts. Traditions that stress a law-governed creation, such as the Reformed, have tended to put creative energies into government and work. The Anabaptist tradition, emphasizing God's provision for human needs, has emphasized work including works of compassion and healing. The evangelical tradition in theology places strong emphasis on sin and grace. This has led to a creative outlet in evangelism and missions.[4]

But we should note that creativity is a cultural capacity to be developed in all persons and not just in an elite minority. Of course, some people are more gifted in the area of creativity than are others. But creativity can be repressed or exalted beyond measure and exercised in irresponsible ways. A creative community can nourish creativity, but it can also become snobbish, self-centered, elitist, and therefore repressive. In summary, creativity exists for the glory of God and for justice and peace and enjoyment among all people.

## The Fall: Voluntary and Tragic

Differences between people are on the surface. Likenesses are deep. All people—rich or poor, wise or foolish, educated or uneducated—breathe the same breath, become hungry and thirsty, eat and drink, sleep, get sick, and die a physical death. Tears and sorrows, gladness and smiles, move us all. We all hope, fear, and love.

Religion has to do with the likenesses in people and not with the surface differences. One of the reasons Christianity is the greatest and the final religion is the fact that it goes straight to the most important likenesses, deals with them, and does not bother with the less important differences.

The apostle Paul, inspired by God, wrote in Romans 3:22 that in regard to the deepest and most important things "there is no difference" (KJV). For Paul, a fundamental fact was that there is no difference in the fact of universal sin.

The section on creation noted that God is perfect. Since the perfect God made humanity, why are we sinful and cut off from our Creator? This is a basic question of Christian theology. In order to answer this question, the Bible does not advance a theory or an abstract philosophy of the origin of evil. Instead it tells the story of how Adam and Eve fell from the perfect relationship with God which they originally had. This story, in Genesis 2 and 3, points to an event right at the beginning of mankind's existence on earth.

### The Fall of Satan and His Angels

*The biblical doctrine of Satan.*—Any study of the fall, based on biblical teaching, should begin with the doctrine of the fall of Satan. This does not mean that the present-day Christian who accepts the biblical teaching concerning Satan is committed to all of the crude imagery that has sprung up around belief in Satan. In the light of medieval and modern distortions, a careful consideration of the biblical teaching concerning Satan is especially needed.

A detailed doctrine of Satan is not found in the Bible until New Testament times. A number of reasons have been suggested for the relatively limited material on Satan in the Old Testament.

God began his self-revelation in the ancient world of polytheism (belief in many gods). God wanted to lead his people to a dynamic practical monotheism (the belief in and worship of one God). Thus, the Old Testament places a primary emphasis on the supremacy of the God of Abraham, Isaac, and Jacob who delivered the Hebrews from Egyptian slavery.

Despite the controversy over such Old Testament passages as Genesis 3:1-19, Isaiah 14:12-15, and Ezekiel 28:12-19, the Bible teaches that from the early moments of the creation of this world Satan was on the scene, a rebel against God. Pride seems to have been the cause of his fall. Following the suggestion in Revelation 12:7-9, the drama of temptation unfolds. Satan came to Adam and Eve disguised as a serpent. He is seen as the agent of temptation for the first man and woman (Gen. 3:10; Rev. 20:2). Although there is not much in the Old Testament about Satan, when he does appear he is the adversary of God's people. He sought to lead God's people into going beyond finite limits (1 Chron. 21:1) or slandered them to God's face (Zech. 3:1).

The most extensive Old Testament discussion of Satan is in Job. Here Satan is seen as God's agent and minister, who tested human fidelity. Satan made a wager with God, with Job as the stake. He acted, however, with the express permission of God and kept within the limits which God fixed for him (Job 1:12; 2:6).

A careful study of the New Testament reveals that the basic message of both Jesus and Paul is closely related to Satanology. The work of Christ is seen as primary in the battle with Satan. Evil is radical and rooted in the personal—it is not just general and abstract in nature. Evil is something with which a person cannot cope within his or her own strength.

In the first three Gospels, Satan is pictured as a supernatural evil spirit who is at the head of a host of inferior evil spirits called demons. As such, he is the "prince of the demons" (Mark 3:22).

The apostle Paul taught that the world was under the heel of celestial world rulers (1 Cor. 2:8; 2 Cor. 4:4; Eph. 6:12). Man is under bondage to evil powers. Salvation is seen in terms of rescue and God's power. Satan is the god of this age (2 Cor. 4:4), whose objective is to keep human beings from believing in the saving power of the gospel. Satan's main objective is to frustrate the redemptive purposes of God.

In Ephesians 6:11-12, Paul stated that the believer's struggle is against the devil and against principalities, authorities, world rulers of this present darkness, and spiritual hosts of wickedness in high places.

The Book of James evidently sees a double source of temptation. One source is the inner nature of man (Jas. 4:1). The other source of temptation is the devil. James warned his readers to "resist the devil and he will flee from you" (4:7). James did not develop the method by which temptation can come from the inner man and from the devil.

One New Testament source for the idea that evil spirits are fallen angels is 2 Peter 2:4. According to Peter, there is a class of angels who sinned and who were therefore cast down into Sheol where they are prisoners until the day of judgment. Another source is Jude 6, which tells of angels who left their proper dwelling and who are kept in eternal chains in the underworld until the judgment of the great day.

An important passage in the Book of Revelation, chapter 12, portrays a vision of the powers that operate in the spiritual world behind the scenes of human history. The red dragon (Satan) is seen as seeking to destroy the woman (a representation of the ideal and historic church) in an age-long battle (v. 3).

In Revelation 12:4, John stated that the tail of the dragon draws a third of the stars of heaven and casts them to the earth. This is usually seen as referring to a primeval war in heaven since stars are familiar symbols of fallen angels.

The biblical materials avoid an ultimate dualism (two coequal powers) which would make Satan equal with God. Neither in the Old Testament nor in the New Testament does this kingdom of evil opposing the kingdom of God become an absolute dualism. The fallen angels are ultimately helpless before the power of God and his angels. Furthermore, in the New Testament, all such spiritual powers are creatures of God and, therefore, ultimately subject to his power.

To hold a doctrine of Satan does not mean that God is less than all powerful or that he is not love. God limited himself in order to give humankind and angels freedom. Obviously, there cannot be freedom unless there is the possibility of decision and rebellion.

The biblical portrayal of evil in a personal form, as in the fallen angel story, avoids both monism (all reality is one) and dualism. It does not place too much emphasis on the power of the demonic but preserves man's responsibility for his sin. The Bible also emphasizes the ultimate power of God and the limitations of Satan and evil.

*Temptation through the serpent.*—We have already seen that man is unique because he is the only creature who is made in the image and likeness of God (Gen. 1:27). Man is so created as male and female that he not only receives his being from God but also determines his being by a free and responsible choice.

Placed in the Garden of Eden, our first parents were told by their Maker that they might eat of all the trees of the Garden save one, the tree of the knowledge of good and evil (Gen. 2:17). Man's glory then is a glory which involves a choice, and the choice implies the awful possibility of failure and misery.

God gave to Adam and Eve the responsibility for obedience, and he also explained the consequences of disobedience. Clearly he did not intend to keep humankind perfect by protecting us from every opportunity to sin. Yet also he had created Adam and Eve with the ability to remain completely free from sin and thus live their lives in obedience to him (Gen. 3:1-3).

God thus prepared the Garden with its tree of the knowledge of good and evil, and he used the tree as an instrument to test man's obedience. Given the power of choice, by obedience to God's plan, man would be established in the righteousness with which he was created.

The temptation, by contrast, was Satan's work. Temptation may be defined as any suggestion or solicitation to do evil. Unlike testing, the aim of temptation is to weaken, degrade, and destroy persons by seducing them from the righteousness with which they were created. Yet, the art of Satan, subtle, deceitful, and malicious as it may be, is not the final cause of man's sin. We cannot find, as Eve tried to do, the excuse for man's sin in his temptation. Of course man was capable—because he was a free and responsible agent—of being tempted. But to be tempted to sin was one thing. To yield to sin is another thing. It was not temptation but man's yielding to temptation that constituted his sin and downfall.

Since the time of the first temptation, man has sought to blame his sin on other persons or on some condition. Modern man consults a psychiatrist to find reasons for his sinful behavior in his past experience. He consults a sociologist to find reasons for his sinful behavior in his environment. But sin, by definition, is a free and responsible act of disobedience.

Even though he may know nothing of the theoretical debate between theologians and philosophers about the nature of sin, every Christian knows in his own experience the truth of the biblical witness that sin is his fault, not his fate. Therefore, according to the Bible, the final solution of sin is repentance, not analysis. This is true whether the analysis be the rational analysis of the social philosopher or the psychoanalysis of the therapist.[5] Try as we may to understand and explain sin, we cannot do so. We can only confess it and repent of it.

**The Fall of Man**

*The nature of the fall.*—The will of God for man was given in terms of the tree of the knowledge of good and evil. God's will for man was stated in the prohibition of the fruit of the tree. To put it very simply, man fell by an act of disobedience. As the apostle Paul said, "For as by one man's disobedience many were made sinners" (Rom. 5:19).

The basic issue in the fall account is not the seemingly harmless act of eating fruit but is found in the violation of God's authority and will portrayed in the prohibition of eating from the tree. This outward act of eating the fruit and expressing revolt reveals a doubting of God's goodness, a disputing of God's wisdom, a disbelief in God's word, and a desire to have the divine rights. The ultimate root of sin has been seen as pride or as unbelief. These causes are relevant not only to the original disobedience of our first parents but also to the continued disobedience of their offspring.

Sin is not passed along as a matter of defective blood or bent genes. Since it is essentially in the moral sphere that we speak of sin, we must understand original sin in personal, not physical, categories. It is better to follow the analogy that Paul himself drew in Romans 5 between Christ and Adam. In Paul's thought, Christ is our Representative who by his life of obedience and sacrificial death in our place redeems us from sin. Thus Christ became the second Adam. To preserve the analogy, then, the first Adam must be thought of as our representative also. He also acted for us. However, in contrast to the second Adam, the first Adam's life was one of disobedience. Therefore, as those who are in Christ are made alive in him, so those who are in Adam are seen as sinners in him (Rom. 5:12-14).

This means, therefore, that sin is basically a spiritual and not a natural defilement, although its infection extends to every part of human nature. Original sin is a spiritual contagion which in some unexplainable way is passed on and becomes rooted in man until he assents to it and allows it to dominate his whole being. Being born in Adam means that we inherit a nature and an environment inclined toward sin. There is no need to teach a child to do wrong; it comes naturally.

Since the fall, despite the inherited tendency to reject God, man has had the power of choice. But we all make the fatal choice of our first parents and sin against God. This biblical emphasis on both inherited tendency and human responsibility is found in Psalm 51:5, "Behold, I was brought forth in iniquity,/and in sin did my mother conceive me" and in Isaiah 53:6, "All we like sheep have gone astray;/we have turned every one to his own way."

This does not mean that all persons descending from Adam are as bad as they could be, but none are as good as they should be. This is a way to understand the doctrine of total depravity. Another way of stating total depravity is by indicating that every part of human nature is affected by the pull toward sin. There is no area within human life where people can always think purely or act rightly.

In summary, total depravity can be thought of as having four meanings, all of which are valid. First, it refers to the corruption at the very center of man's being, the heart. But this does not mean that man's humanity has ceased to exist. Second, it signifies the infection in every part of man's being. But this is not to infer that this infection is evenly distributed or that nothing good remains. Third, it denotes the total inability of sinful man to please God or come to him unless moved by grace. But this does not imply that man is not free in other areas of life. Fourth, it includes the idea of the universal corruption of the human race. This is true despite the fact that some peoples and cultures manifest this corruption much less than others. The universality of sin was noted by the apostle Paul: "None is righteous, no, not one. All have sinned and fall short of the glory of God" (Rom. 3:10,23).[6]

Based on their understanding of biblical teachings, many Evangelicals believe that until a person actualizes his inherited Adam way of life in personal rebellion, he is within the provision of the redemptive work of the second Adam—Jesus Christ. No one will be lost just because of an inherited nature and environment inclined toward sin. Up to the point of positive transgression or rejection of moral light at the age of accountability, the individual is "provided for" in the grace of God without personal repentance and faith.

When the child does reach the age of responsibility or accountability, his only hope is to be led immediately to turn from the Adam way of life to Jesus Christ as his Sin-bearer and Savior. One does not come into the Christian life by chance or automatically as the result of teaching or nurture. The basic human problem is not just ignorance but rebellion against God. One comes into the Christian life in response to the call of God through a conscious choice and surrender of life to Jesus Christ.

Although it need not be a highly emotional experience, this entrance into the Christian life must be a conscious response of the individual to God's provision in Jesus Christ. This is one reason evangelical people have outreach programs, personal witnessing, decision services, and revivals.

First Corinthians 7:14 teaches that children born into a Christian household do have some relation to the body of Christ which infants born of pagans do not possess. Even if the child has only one Christian parent, there is still a special holiness or influence brought into his or her life. Perhaps this teaching undergirds the value of a public infant dedication service. Of course, neither the husband nor the child is saved in an evangelical Christian sense by virtue of this holiness of the Christian wife and mother (1 Cor. 7:16). Belief in Jesus Christ is that which one does for oneself (Rom. 10:9 *ff.*).

*The consequences of the fall.*—Sin and the fall alienate man from God. Overwhelmed with a sense of guilt and shame, Adam and Eve hid themselves from the face of their Maker. Made in and for fellowship with God, they ran from him who was the source of their highest good. Their eyes were opened and they were naked and they hid themselves from the presence of the Lord God among the trees of the garden (Gen. 3:8).

It is interesting that this sense of exposure should focus on the sex organs. The suggestion has been made that this is due to the fact that in the sex act man spawns sinful descendants. In this regard note the Old Testament ritual of the cleansing of a mother who gives birth with a sin offering (Lev. 12:6-8). This may be the ritual equivalent of the psalmist's confession, "Behold I was brought forth in iniquity,/and in sin did my mother conceive me" (Ps. 51:5).

Sin and the fall bring God's wrath upon man. This rebellion does not mean that God's nature changes. The change is in man, not God. Because God is a holy God, he cannot relate to fallen man as he originally related to unfallen man.

Instead of harmony there is now anger which expresses itself in condemnation and a curse. This curse does not remove the privileges and responsibilities with which man is created but rather embitters and distorts them. Motherhood is now involved with pain. Work is related to toil and perspiration. The relationship of man and woman is marred (Gen. 3:16-20).

In the realm of personality, man lost his capacity to know himself accurately and to determine his own course of action freely in response to his intelligence. Man's intelligence also became impaired. Now he can no longer gain a fully accurate knowledge of the world around him, nor is he able to reason without constantly falling into error. Morally, man became less able to discern good and evil. Socially, he began to exploit his fellowmen. Creatively, his imagination became separated from reality. The fullest biblical statement of these ideas is in Romans 1—2.

The consequences of God's wrath can be seen in the corrupt condition in society, as well as in the realm of personality. An example is the way in which David corrupted the institutions of marriage and government, multiplied abuses of political power, and trapped servants and soldiers by implicating them. This continued until the Word of God awakened his conscience. But David could not go back and fully correct the social corruption and harm he had done to persons.

In our time, we can give numerous examples of the consequences of God's wrath. Instead of seeking wholeness and harmony as brothers and sisters, people in society tend to exploit each other wherever possible. Groups with powerful influence in society, such as trade unions and professional associations, often pursue their own interests under the slogan of justice. But when we look for justice for our own group alone, we are willing injustice for others.[7]

This biblical doctrine of the fall is in opposition to the enlightenment view of "secular humanism" and certain groups of the religious right who want to remove restraint from the powerful, confident that their native goodness will not be a threat to the weak. The Bible states that sin even persists in the life of the elect. Even after we become Christians, we struggle to fulfill our Christian calling in a life of love and justice. The sin of lust for godlike power described in Genesis is oftentimes more fundamental and serious than sins related to sexuality.

Sin and the fall pervert man's entire environment. In the fall, the very ground was affected adversely for man's sake (Gen. 3:17). As Paul said, the whole creation groans and travails again until now (Rom. 8:22). The Genesis account of man's fall talks of thorns and thistles that turn work into toil. The created order is spoiled. Nature is red in tooth and claw. Earthquakes, floods, and famines destroy human life. The Bible links these to the fall, but it does not explain exactly how the one has caused the other.

Sometimes men and women treat nature as an enemy to subdue and exploit instead of a trust to nurture and develop. We probe and use its resources with no thought for the effects that a wrong use of nature might have. Rather than being good stewards and entering into community with the birds of the air, the beasts of the wood, and the flowers of the field, we pollute the atmosphere, rape the land, and upset the animal world with our unfeeling attacks on the environment. Humanity sets itself against itself and nature, as well as against God.

There is a growing awareness that resources are running down, pollution is growing, and technology is escalating out of control. This has given birth to a whole literature and movement calling for proper and human use of the limited resources on planet earth. It stresses simpler styles of living, less waste, and a closer relationship with and respect for nature. This new awareness is in keeping with the biblical teaching.

Sin and the fall bring death. God had given Adam and Eve the warning that should they defy the divine prohibition and eat the forbidden fruit, they would die. After their rebellion this warning became a reality. They were banished from the Garden with its tree of life. They—and we their offspring—face the fearful prospect of returning to the ground from which we were taken. The phrase "for dust thou art, and unto dust shalt thou return" (Gen. 3:19, KJV) is no mere description of a natural process. Death in the Bible is anything but a "natural" phenomenon. Death is that last enemy who can only be destroyed by Christ who rose from the dead.

The consequences of the fall are spelled out in Genesis 4—11. The rebellion which Adam and Eve initiated grew increasingly worse in the accounts in Genesis 4—11. When Cain killed his brother Abel, brotherly hatred entered history, and the disruption which was present between the parents spread through the whole family (Gen. 4).

At this point in our story, we read of the growth of culture (Gen. 4:17-24). There is the mention of the first city, of cattle herders, and of musicians. But when the smith is introduced, the result of his work is Lamech's terrible sword of vengeance (Gen. 4:23-24). The disruption caused by man's rebellion had spread through humankind.

The disruption caused by the fall even invaded the divine realm. In Genesis 6:1-4 the sons of the gods take to themselves for wives the daughters of men. The result of this union are the Nephilim, the giants, a demonic race of supermen, in which the divine vitality is mixed with the human. These giants have the possibility of living forever and therefore of challenging God's sovereignty. God's judgment upon them was to limit their life span to 120 years and to relegate them to the realm of mortal men (v. 3).

In all probability, the "sons of God" in Genesis 6 are angelic beings, just as they are in Job. In fact, they could well be the angels of Jude 6, who "did not keep their own position but left their proper dwelling." Just as the serpent tempted Eve, now deviant divine beings corrupted humankind. Man was being troubled by something outside himself which could not be representative of a holy God, something surely demonic.

Genesis thus points out that man is thoroughly corrupted. His rebellion spread so that it even invaded the heavenly realm. As it is put so well in Genesis 6:5-6, "Every imagination of the thoughts of his heart was only evil continually. And the Lord was sorry that he had made man on the earth, and it grieved him to his heart." The one recourse left to God was to blot out the creation.

God's mercy came into play at that point. Noah and his family were saved in the ark, along with representatives of every living creature. And God himself even shut the door of the ark after Noah (Gen. 7:16), just to make sure it was tightly sealed. When his wrath was expended, God "remembered" Noah (Gen. 8:1) and carefully restored the order to creation, promising that while the earth remains the seasons and harvest and day and night will never cease (Gen. 8:22). He also promised that the primeval chaos would never again rise to threaten the existence of the world (Gen. 9:8-17).

But even this mercy did not stop the corruption. At the tower of Babel (Gen. 11:1-9), humankind came to its ultimate rebellion. All nations united together in a cooperative venture. Their unity would seem good on the face of it, but their goal was still revolt. Here no longer was man completely dependent on his Creator. He was a rebel storming the heights of heaven in order to create his own glory. His perfection, he thought, was not his likeness to God but his ability to replace God. His task was not to serve God but to make God unnecessary. From Eden to Babel, humankind had not learned a thing. In his judgment at Babel, God dispersed people throughout the earth and confused human language, in order that people may never again cooperatively challenge the Lord of the world (Gen. 11:7-9). The possibility of human relationships was replaced by confusion. Revolt against God led inevitably to the disruption of human society. Thus all history is marked by the twin tragedies of sin and death.[8]

### The Fall and Natural Science

The account of the fall of man, as it comes to us in the Bible, speaks as of an event occurring a few thousand years ago in a geographical setting located in the ancient Near East. Few Bibles published today show the classic chronology of Bishop Ussher which dates the creation of man in 4004 BC. Despite the fact that the fall of man was a real occurrence, we do not expect to find a biblical atlas that would locate the Garden of Eden on a technical map, as it does Ur of the Chaldees and the city of Jerusalem.

In the light of these developments, many have suggested that the Adam-Eve story is a myth. However, the analogy between Adam and Christ shows us how impossible it is to completely relate the primal history of Genesis *only* to experience and be faithful to Scripture. The life, death, and resurrection of Christ took place in time and space. He was crucified under Pontius Pilate. In our Christian calling, to be sure, the Holy Spirit makes us contemporary with Christ. But we become contemporaries not of a myth or idea but of a historical event, indeed, a historical person. Man's salvation is not only a matter of present experience but of past history.

Of course, the writers of Scripture knew little of the vast periods of time with which modern physical anthropologists work any more than they knew of the even more vast periods of cosmic time involved in the creation of heaven and Earth. They likely thought of the creation and fall of man as occurring in the relatively recent past in the cradle of civilization, the Tigris-Euphrates Valley. The authors of Scripture, the human organs of inspiration and revelation, were not simply translated out of their own times and culture in terms of technical history, anthropology, and astronomy. Had they been so, their message would have been meaningless to their contemporaries. Therefore the Bible account of man's creation and fall comes down to us in a form that reflects the historical and cultural background of the times in which the documents were produced. This does not, however, distort its basic meaning and reality.

It is also true that we do not have the precise historical and technical material concerning the details of time and space as far as the first Adam is concerned that we have with reference to the work of the second Adam, Jesus Christ. But it is the reality of the historical fall and the revealed meaning of that historical event, not the technical details of time and place, that are important to Christian faith in understanding the fall.

The same is true for the salvation event. It does not matter that we do not know the exact year that Jesus was born, the exact chronological sequence of his public ministry, nor exactly how to arrange the geographical details of the resurrection appearances. The revealed theological meaning and the historical reality of Jesus' life, death, and resurrection are the matters of crucial importance to Christian faith. And so it is with the primal history of the race, which is that history back of Abraham which is not open to technical historical investigation and control. But this history controls us as Christians. As we accept by faith the inspired account and interpretation of its reality and inner meaning, it illuminates our present and our future with a saving light.

## God's Common Grace and Providence

There is some justification for introducing the doctrines of common grace and providence immediately after a discussion of the fall. Common grace is the care that God takes of all existing things. After the fall, the grace of preservation was declared to be at work in God's creation. God set boundaries to the destructive impulses and effects of the fall. We remember that after the Flood, God chose to restore the order to creation. He promised that the seasons and harvest and day and night would never cease (Gen. 8:22). He also promised that the flood would never again rise to threaten the world (Gen. 9:8-17).

This doctrine of providential care punishes the wicked (in a broad sense) (Rom. 1:18), supports the weak, and directs history (including the lives of persons and nations) within the context of freedom toward the divine purpose. Common grace is God's goodness to all people in extending so widely the gifts of his creation and in restraining evil as extensively as he does. This common or general grace of God keeps life human and sustains the earth. It accounts for sinful man's ability to arrive at some justice. Common grace is the grace of preservation by which man's tendency to destroy is restrained. Indeed, if it were not for common grace, the world would fall into complete lawlessness and disorder.

But God preserves his created order out of his mercy. Common grace, together with the reflection of the glory of God in created human nature, is responsible for the fragments of wisdom and truth that exist in the non-Christian religions and in the moral codes of the great civilizations of pagan antiquity.

## Common Grace

Common or general grace applies to everyone alive. This is because it comes from God's universal fatherhood. His grace is received by us all as we share in the many blessings of life. Through our sin we have lost any claim on him, yet he still gives abundant tokens of his generosity and goodness day by day. These gifts are showered on all, regardless of creed, character, or color.

Perhaps the clearest expression of God's common grace is seen in the fact that he preserves some truth and morality among people. Everyone keeps some sense of what is true, good, and beautiful.

Paul saw a further result of this common grace. It helps to open people's hearts and minds to the goodness of God and so prepares them to receive God's special grace in Jesus Christ (Acts 16:27-30).

## Providence

Providence is both personal, as in the inner voice of conscience, and corporate, as in the judgments of history and the laws of nature. When the structures of nature meet us in judgment or buoy us up in grace, it is the providence of God being confronted. We are meeting One who put down the mighty from their thrones and exalted those of low degree (Luke 1:52).

*General Providence.*—Providence includes the orders of general preservation, such as the state (Rom. 13), human work, and the family. Sin's broad extent does not mean that no good deeds are done. The Creator remains the living God, active in the world in spite of sin and pursuing good purposes still. Christians can thus rightly speak of common grace and the goodness of God that causes the deeds of wrathful men to praise him so that human relationships, society, and culture are in some measure constructive. Governments and workers, artists and teachers, parents and friends, sinful as they be, may continue to serve God's purposes whether they acknowledge it or not.

In fact, God blesses those countries which live by the light of the moral laws of general revelation and the orders of preservation and brings down judgment on nations which violate these laws and orders (Prov. 14:34). The rules of business and trade are accountable to God. The family is a divinely instituted design, and the weakening of it through sexual immorality and critical attack is harmful to the general order of humanity. These elementary norms, which make and keep life human, are accessible through general revelation and common grace. God passes out justice and judgment to those who tear the fabric that providence so carefully preserves.

The framework of government is ordained by God. The state, however, can move outside its proper responsibilities. The Bible is wary about the pretensions of government. Revelation 13, with its vision of the beast, must be held in tension with Romans 13, which praises the institution of government. When the state becomes demonic, it must be resisted, as the early Christians did when they refused to worship the emperor of Rome. God's good gifts to us, including the very orders of preservation, can be corrupted by sin. The reason for including government in the doctrine of providence is because it can restrain the imperial drives of human sin and assure the well-being of human life together in a fallen world.

Sensitive biblical students see a departure from orthodox biblical doctrine when it is stated that there should be a removal of restraints to man's imperial drives toward political and economic power. The tradition that government has a purpose to protect the weak from greed and control the dominating tendencies of the strong seems to be an extension of biblical teaching. In fact, there are many political and economic implications in the teaching of Christ. He began his ministry with the announcement of good news for the poor. Christ further preached concerned love for the victim and criticized the rich for injustice and greed.

*Personal providence.*—Providence does not merely work in the broad stretches of nature and history and in the boundaries set to the rebellion of the world. There is also a tender and individual care that numbers the hairs of our heads and marks the sparrow's fall (Matt. 10:29-31). The eye of faith sees the hand of God laboring to shape our personal lives toward "wise and loving ends." Indeed the meanings to be found in one's personal life do not come easily. Providence struggles with "thrones and authorities" who are only too eager to shoot down the sparrow and bruise the head. Yet the light that comes from Jesus Christ and the knowledge that the powers of this fallen world do not have final charge of our destinies, illuminates even those events whose darkness seems difficult to penetrate (Rom. 8:28,37-39).

*The nature of God and providence.*—The ways in which we see providence work depends to a large extent on how we understand God. It makes a big difference whether we think of God the Creator personally or impersonally. If the Creator is not viewed personally, the focus will be on nature and with broad generalizations which have to do with natural explanations. There will be little place for providence in history, in miracles, and in personal life. But if the providential God is seen as the personal Creator, his goodness will be seen in what he does within time—in the intimacy of personal experiences and in historical actions.

Such a God will be one who enters into persons' lives, who responds to prayers and who suffers and rejoices with human beings. In spite of humankind's disobedience and the cosmic consequences of sin upon creation, the providence of God in his acts of goodness works for the sustaining of creation as well as for its redemption.

According to Karl Barth, history is composed of both the confusion of humanity and the providence of God. Because God is creator of heaven and earth and the Father of our Lord Jesus Christ, history is unraveling according to God's fatherly providence. If, on the other hand, we try to make sense out of history from our human perspective we primarily see confusion. God's providential guidance of history cannot be charted on a technical graph. Rather his providence is an affirmation based on biblical revelation.

How, then, is the Christian to live in a world that on the surface is marked by confusion but that underneath is guided by the providence of God? Each morning Christians are to pick themselves up and take a few more steps on their pilgrim way. They know that they cannot decipher a neat little plan of the providence of God, for what they see in the daily paper is the confusion of humanity. Yet they believe that deeper than the daily news is the providence of God. For themselves they have found the meaning of their lives and therefore of history in Jesus Christ. This is true because the secret meaning of history is to be found in God's purposes in Jesus Christ.

### Notes

1. James W. Sire, *The Universe Next Door* (Downers Grove, IL: InterVarsity Press, 1976), p. 25.
2. Robin Keeley, ed., *Eerdmans' Handbook to Christian Belief* (Grand Rapids, MI: Eerdmans, 1982), p. 219.

3. Ibid., p. 236. Tertullian, the early church father, made a well-known attack on women.

4. Arthur F. Holmes, *Contours of a World View* (Grand Rapids, MI: Eerdmans, 1983), pp. 202-206.

5. Paul King Jewett, "Original Sin and the Fall of Man," *Southwestern Journal of Theology,* Vol. 19, No. 1 (Fall 1976): 19-21.

6. Donald G. Bloesch, *Essentials of Evangelical Theology,* Vol. 1: *God, Authority, & Salvation* (San Francisco: Harper & Row, 1978), p. 90.

7. Gabriel Fackre, *The Religious Right and Christian Faith* (Grand Rapids, MI: Eerdmans, 1982), p. 49.

8. Jewett, pp. 25-26. Cf. Achtemeier.

## Bibliography

Achtemeier, Paul J. and Elizabeth. *The Old Testament Roots of Our Faith.* Nashville: Abingdon Press, 1962.

Bloesch, Donald G. *Essentials of Evangelical Theology.* Vol. 1: *God, Authority, & Salvation.* San Francisco: Harper & Row, 1978.

Fackre, Gabriel. *The Christian Story.* Grand Rapids, MI: Eerdmans, 1978.

_____. *The Religious Right and Christian Faith.* Grand Rapids, MI: Eerdmans, 1982.

Holmes, Arthur F. *Contours of a World View.* Grand Rapids, MI: Eerdmans, 1983.

Jewett, Paul King. "Original Sin and the Fall of Man." *Southwestern Journal of Theology,* Vol. 19, No. 1 (Fall 1976): 19-21.

Keeley, Robin, ed. *Eerdmans' Handbook to Christian Belief.* Grand Rapids, MI: Eerdmans, 1982.

Newport, John P. *Christianity and Contemporary Art Forms.* Waco: Word, Inc., 1971.

_____. *Demons, Demons, Demons.* Nashville: Broadman Press, 1972.

_____. "The Theology and Experience of Salvation." *The Greek Orthodox Theological Review,* Vol. XXII, No. 4 (Winter 1977): 393-404.

Ramm, Bernard. *After Fundamentalism: The Future of Evangelical Theology.* San Francisco: Harper & Row, 1983.

Sire, James W. *The Universe Next Door.* Downers Grove, IL: InterVarsity Press, 1976.

# 7
# Jesus Christ, the Redeemer, and Salvation

## God's Election and Covenant: The Redemptive Beginning

Recently a dialogue was held between theologians. A prominent professor stated, "You should thank God every time you pass a Jewish synagogue because it reminds us of the beginnings of God's redemptive purpose in history through Abraham and the Jews." Another person present asked, "Do you mean that the redemptive truth for all men began through a particular people?" The answer was "Yes."

Still another person asked, "Why did the special redemptive knowledge of God arise only in Israel in the ancient world?" The answer was, "This is the mystery of election and covenant and the independent will and purpose of God." The fact is that only in Israel did the unique concepts of election and covenant arise and develop and prepare the way for Jesus Christ and the redemption of humankind.

The universal common grace and providence of God, which sustains and preserves all of creation from its self-destructive tendencies, has been noted. In Genesis 12, the Bible moves to the particular channel of God's redemptive actions. God promised to bless the world through the descendants of Abraham. In other words, God chose to work through a special people to achieve his eternal purpose. With Israel, God established a covenant: the vision would shine before Israel as a pillar of fire, and the people would follow it.[1] God was to deliver his people from bondage and give them a vision of the salvation for which the world was made. The guidelines for that life are set forth in the Ten Commandments, the wisdom of the sages, and in the hopes of the prophets. The covenant love which would not let this people go, even in the face of their rebellion, found fulfillment in Israel's Prophet, Priest, and King, Jesus Christ.

It will be helpful to look in detail at the way in which God began his redemptive work in history. We can understand this remarkable love plan best in terms of the biblical concepts of election and covenant.

## Election

Election means that God chose a people through whom he would achieve his plan in history. We need to see how this concept of election arose, what was and was not meant by it, and the purpose and history of it.

God had many people, but he reserved a special love for Israel. This love expressed itself in election (Gen. 12:1-3). This is the chief clue for the understanding of the meaning and significance of Israel. Many have objected to this idea of election. They say that the God of love and justice could hardly exhibit such favoritism. But we must remember that Israel paid a terrible price for this election. Israel was not elected just to receive special privilege. God was often in conflict with the natural desires of Israel. Amos 3:2 states, "You only have I known . . ./therefore I will punish you/for all your iniquities."

It must also be said that Israel was not chosen because of merit. Then why did God choose Israel? Israel found this purpose in the promise to the patriarchs. God had delivered Israel because God remembered his covenant with Abraham, with Isaac, and with Jacob (Ex. 2:24). God brought Israel up out of Egypt because he had promised to make them a nation. God set Israel free in the wilderness to start the march toward the Promised Land (Lev. 25:38; Deut. 6:23; Ps. 105).

Included in this promise to the patriarchs is the oath to bring blessing on all nations through Israel, and this purpose Israel saw as the ultimate reason for its own redemption and creation as a nation. God's son, Israel, was brought out of Egypt for God's purpose of redeeming all human-kind. Israel was set free from the house of bondage to be the means whereby God would restore to persons the righteous life that he had given them in creation. This good life they had lost by their rebellion. In the event of the Exodus, God continued to work to restore this righteous life to mankind.

When God created Israel, he began literally to recreate his world, fashioning the means whereby rebellious people might be restored to the good life they had lost (Isa. 51:9-11). God loved and chose Israel in order that Israel might serve him and in order that through Israel he might bestow his love upon all. God loves Israel because he loves humankind (1 Tim. 2:3-4).

Why this people Israel in this time and this place? As already indicated, here we confront a puzzle, the mystery of divine election. The Fertile Crescent where Israel was located was just the right place to carry on an experiment in faithfulness. Israel was centrally located on a Mediterranean land bridge. It was a prey of imperialists and the pawn of political disputes. For God's mission, he needed the sturdiest and the most stubborn. Our speculations fade into silence, replaced by our thanksgiving that God also is a stubborn God who will not give up on us.

So the freedom and privileges of election are limited by the independent purposes of God. Not all of the biblical writers saw clearly the universal aim of God for Israel or the mission of Israel for the saving of the nations. Yet all the biblical writers were conscious of the responsibility that went along with Israel's privileges.

### Covenant

The concept of covenant is another foundational element in the redemptive purpose of God. Only after the doctrine of election has been seen as the primary act of God's grace can we see the meaning of the covenant. A covenant is a solemn promise to fulfill a declared purpose. It has to do with the divine promise to keep the divine purpose.

The doctrine of election found its concrete expression in the Old Testament concept of covenant. God offered a compact out of grace. This compact had advantages for Israel: an inheritance; security from enemies; and law, order, and inner peace. Acceptance of the covenant meant the obligation to obey God. It was not to be seen as a legal burden because law and ethical guidelines were based on God's grace.

When the Israelites were delivered from bondage and set free in the wilderness, they had no idea how to conduct themselves in their new life. The picture we have in Exodus 16—18 is one of a confused multitude, uncertain in their trust of their newfound Redeemer and undecided as how to get along with one another and with their God. This situation was soon changed by the structuring of Israel's life in a covenant community. The covenant made at Mount Sinai with *Yahweh* (God), defined the Israelites' relationship to one another and to their God. In short, the covenant defined the nature of Israel's service to the Lord.

Primary to the covenant relationship was the fact that *Yahweh* was to be Israel's sole and sovereign Lord. He was to rule over his people, and they were to serve him alone. Such is the essential meaning of the first four of the Ten Commandments (Ex. 20:3-11). At the foot of Mount Sinai, Israel was given a choice. Having been delivered by *Yahweh,* Israel was asked to serve *Yahweh* alone.

Israel's decision was not to be made in a vacuum. The people had seen what *Yahweh* could do and how *Yahweh* had overcome the Egyptians (Ex. 17:8-16). The Israelites had been in the desert and God had given them water and food (Ex. 15:22 to 16:36) and had proved himself constantly gracious. *Yahweh* had taken the initiative, and Israel was being asked to respond to his graces (Ex. 19:4-6).

The covenant which Israel was asked to make with *Yahweh* at Mount Sinai was no pact between equals however. Israel was not being asked to be God's partner. The Israelites were being asked to surrender, to give *Yahweh* full charge of their lives, of their loyalty, and of their destiny. This meant that, if the people entered into covenant relationship with God, God's will forever after was to be the center of their existence.

And this fact had several implications for Israel's life in the world. *First,* unlike all the surrounding cultures of the ancient Near East, Israel's task would no longer be one of adjusting to the natural environment. The ancient Sumerians, Assyrians, Egyptians, and Canaanites found their gods in nature. And it was for the purpose of regulating and appeasing and harmonizing nature that religion lived in these cultures. But Israel was now being asked to surrender to a power outside nature. God had revealed himself through the medium of historical events, especially the Exodus from Egypt, and his will was not to be found in nature but in historical revelation and through his actions and his spoken word.

*Secondly,* if Israel entered into covenant relationship with *Yahweh,* it could not find the center of its life in any human culture. God demanded of this people that they conform not to human laws and ethics and social standards but to his divine and gracious will (Lev. 18:2-4).

*America and the covenant*—As an aside, we should note that the functional elevation of America to the place of a chosen nation is not in the Bible. The United States shares with all people the universal covenants of Adam and Noah and a status and role in the order of preservation.[2] The historical influence exerted on America by the biblical vision of liberty and justice for all under God makes America accountable to

God in a special way. But there is only one covenant stream in the Bible through which God does his special work of redemption.

The confusion of a secular state with a special election of God has problems. It feeds the flames of nationalism while at the same time dampening internal criticism. The absence of the sense of prophetic judgment on our nation and the lack of a biblical understanding of human nature show up in superpatriotism and a self-righteous fury. The United States stands under the same prophetic judgment and has people of a fallen nature as its citizens as do all other nations.

*Israel and responsibility under the covenant.*—As an example of the responsibility of being an elect and covenant nation, in Israel there was to be an equality of persons in the law. The poor, weak, and defenseless received unique consideration. God was for the weak and was a terror to the rich and wicked. This, then, was to be the nature of the covenant service into which Israel was asked to enter. And when the demands which God had spoken to Moses on the mountain were heard, the Israelites made their choice and dedicated themselves to the Lord: "All the words which the Lord has spoken we will do" (Ex. 24:3; 19:7-8). Of their own free will, Israel agreed to be God's chosen people. There follows in Exodus 24:4-11 the description of the covenant ceremony certifying or symbolizing this agreement and response.

*Christians and the covenant.*—The important point for Christians to see, however, is that the service laid upon Israel is also ours. We are called into the covenant community. In the context of the grace of God in Jesus Christ's life, death, and resurrection, we are asked to make our decision. But if we decide to give our lives to the Lord, to enter into the new covenant as members of his church, we surrender our own wills and become responsible to God alone. No longer is our task to adjust to our world or to our society. Our mission is to become obedient to a will transcending them both. And our pledge is to live as faithful members of God's community of salvation which is the church.

### Uniqueness of Meaning, Destiny, and Purpose

Election and covenant are the chief clues for understanding Israel's sense of destiny and meaning for existence. These concepts are not found in other countries. Even when Israel got a king, he was adopted as God's son to protect the people from enemies and secure the social order in righteousness (Ps. 89:19-25). When the kings betrayed this trust, it was said that God would raise up an Anointed One who would fulfill the theological conditions on which the monarchy rested.

Kingship for the Hebrews was not divinely ordained as a primary office but was introduced as an emergency. The ideal or normative period was the kingless period of the wilderness when they lived directly under God's leadership.

In summary, the doctrines of election and covenant gave Israel an interpretation of life and a view of human history which are absolutely fundamental to the structure of Christian theology, especially when they are seen with Christ as their fulfillment.

In the prophets, Israel's theological understanding deepened; but this depth development took place within the covenant. Sin and judgment came. There was longing for the wilderness days when God's people lived directly under God. Yet the prophets felt that God was reliable and would keep his promises. They looked to the future for their fulfillment. For the Christian, this redemptive beginning is brought to a climax and fulfillment in Jesus Christ.

## Jesus Christ: The Redemptive Center and Climax

While studying in India, I found that the Hindus accepted the divinity of Christ but looked upon him as just one of many incarnations or revelations of God. Official guides in the Soviet Union have tried in various ways to explain Jesus. One guide said that Jesus was the product of the wishful thinking by the lower classes of people who yearned for liberation. Other guides said that he was a leader of the oppressed and exploited masses. They further stated that faith in the redeeming work of Christ developed gradually out of the frustration of the working masses who were unable to change their conditions. Other Russians follow Lenin's view which states that Jesus never existed and was a mythical invention.[3]

But for those of us who are Christians, the redemptive acts of God reached their climax and fulfillment in Jesus and the events of Bethlehem, Galilee, Calvary, and Easter. The most crucial part of Christian doctrine relates to the person and work of Jesus Christ. For sake of clarity, in this discussion, the person and work of Christ will be separated. But in reality, the person and work of Christ cannot be separated.

Who he *is* and what he has *done* belong together. One theologian has said that the "*work* of Jesus Christ *is* the *person* of Jesus Christ *in motion.*"

### The Person of Jesus Christ

The New Testament furnishes basic materials for understanding the person of Christ. An important part of the New Testament teaching on the person of Christ was discussed in chapter 4. The technical doctrine of Christ's person was more fully developed, however, by early Christian theologians in answer to heresies.

*The humanity and deity of Jesus.*—On the one hand, the Docetists overspiritualized Jesus. For them, he was not really human. They divorced Jesus from the ordinary world of things, matter, and time. The Council of Chalcedon in 451 responded to this heresy by asserting the *humanity* of the Son of God. On the other hand, the Ebionites reduced Jesus to the human level and denied that he was "very God of very God." In answer, the Chalcedonian Creed declared the *deity* of Jesus Christ. Then the Council affirmed that Christ was one person in two natures without division or confusion. The early councils thus declared that Jesus Christ is truly God, truly human, and truly one.

Evangelical Christians believe that by and large these statements by the early councils are based on the New Testament testimony.

*The characteristics of Jesus as described in the New Testament.*—The New Testament clearly states that the early followers of Christ knew Jesus in the following ways.

*First,* Jesus was a *real* man. Despite critics who have denied that Jesus existed, the Jesus-myth theory is seldom used now by those attempting to discredit Christianity. Jesus existed as a real member of the human race.

*Second,* Jesus was a *unique* man. Jesus was unique because of his message, his actions, and the way he summoned his hearers to follow him exclusively. Perhaps the most forceful way Jesus expressed this was when he claimed that a person's ultimate destiny depended on his attitude toward himself. He said that anybody who acknowledged him as the Messiah would be accepted at the last judgment and anybody who denied him would be condemned (John 3:36).

The friends of Jesus in the early days of his ministry must have wondered just what all that meant. It is difficult to say how much they came to believe about him during his lifetime before his resurrection.

They were prepared to commit themselves to him. They left their homes and families to share in his work. Peter was the first to express his formal belief that Jesus was the Messiah (Matt. 16:13-20).

*Third,* Jesus was *raised from the dead.* Christianity could not have come into being unless Jesus had really existed. Neither would it have come into being unless people had believed in his resurrection as a historical event. The best evidence for the resurrection is the rise of the Christian church. Nothing less than the resurrection could have turned the despondent and disillusioned followers of Jesus into a joyful and vigorous church. The historical resurrection stands on solid ground (1 Cor. 15:3-8). As a result of the resurrection, the early church came to the conclusion that the Jesus whom they had known as a unique earthly man was indeed the Messiah, the Lord, and the Son of God (Rom. 1:1-6).

*Fourth,* Jesus was a *living presence.* To those first Christians, Jesus was not simply a figure of the past. Though physically absent, he was still alive. And if alive, active (John 14:25-26). Also, they saw Jesus, whom they had known as a man, to be a spiritual, universal being. He was no longer a person confined to one place and time. After the resurrection, he could be with all his people everywhere and could enter into a personal relationship with each of them.

*Fifth,* Jesus was a *coming king.* The early Christians knew Jesus to be living with them in the present. They were also concerned about being with him in a more concrete way in the future. He had taught that he would come again with the glory of a king. They confidently expected his return at the end of the world, which they believed was not far distant. They saw him triumphing over all forces of evil and establishing his kingdom before handing over his authority to God the Father (1 Cor. 15:24).

The end of the world has not in fact come as quickly as the first Christians hoped and expected. Some of the New Testament writers themselves faced up to these problems about timing and recognized that God had never laid down any precise time for the return of Jesus (Matt. 24:27,36). They stated that perhaps the coming of Jesus was delayed in God's mercy in order to give more time for people to hear and respond to the gospel (Matt. 24:14). Certainly the end of the world would come when it was least expected, calling for a state of readiness (1 Thess. 5:1-6; Matt. 24:42-44).

Furthermore, we see that the New Testament writers saw Jesus as the fulfillment of Jewish hopes for a Messiah, as the Son of God and as the Lord of creation (Luke 1:31-33; Col. 1:16-17). Paul and John and other New Testament writers affirmed the unique relationship of Jesus with God the Father and God the Spirit (John 14:16,20,26; 15:26; Matt. 28:19; 2 Cor. 13:14; Gal. 4:4-6). From this information in the Bible, the details of the doctrines of the Trinity and the Incarnation were worked out by theologians in the early centuries.

In contemporary life, many Christological reconsiderations openly call into question the classical affirmations about the deity and singularity of Christ. On the other hand, there are those who perhaps unconsciously tend to revive the ancient heresies. The suspicion of the human body and the teaching that sexual sins are the primary forms of human sin are influenced by the Gnostic belief that the flesh is evil. Those who hold this view deny in practice the full humanity of Jesus. The otherworldly or escapist tendencies of some teachings about last things play down the reality and seriousness of this world and this time which the incarnation of Jesus in human flesh validates.

### The Work of Christ

The uniqueness of Jesus Christ concerns more than his person. His incomparable work on the cross is also unique. This means that Christ, as divinity, entered into the human condition, taking upon himself the sin and guilt of the world (2 Cor. 5:19). He was more than a prophet or holy man. Christ was also a sin bearer and mediator between God and humans. He was not only the model or example but also the Savior of a fallen humanity (1 Pet. 2:18-19).

The idea of Jesus as the crucified God is a stumbling block to Jews and folly to Gentiles (1 Cor. 1:23). Maharishi Yogi refuses to consider that Christ ever suffered or that Christ could suffer. Maharishi teaches that through Transcendental Meditation a sinner very easily comes out of the field of sin and becomes a virtuous person. Muhammed taught that Jesus was never crucified but that another took his place. Buddhists, too, find it difficult to come to terms with the crucified Christ. So we see that there is a great gulf between the Christian view of Christ's vicarious or sacrificial work and the view of other religions or cultic groups.[4]

The incarnation of Christ exists for the atonement. The atonement achieved on the cross was a deed done to save us from sin and its consequences. Christ lived for us and he died for us, doing for us what we could not do.

Evangelicals find in the Bible, as did John Calvin, that Jesus Christ is our Priest, Prophet, and King. Thus Christ fulfills the three dominant leadership roles in the Old Testament.

*The priestly role comes into focus in the sacrifice Christ made on the cross.*—*First,* at the cross, Jesus Christ satisfied the *penalty* for human guilt by taking the punishment due to humanity (Gal. 3:13). The blood of Jesus Christ cleanses from sin. This is true because as the God-man he participated in the finite reality on which the curse must fall. As his death satisfied the punishment for our disobedience, his life satisfied the requirements of the perfect obedience expected of us.

At the heart of Christ's substitutionary work is the holiness of God. God is revealed as holy. This means that in a moral universe the penalty for sin must be exacted and the obedience secured.

This emphasis on sin, wrath, and judgment is a corrective to those who overemphasize God's love. God's love is important, but God is also holy. The race is fallen, and a righteous God does hold us accountable for our rebellion.

*Second,* at the cross, the love of God dealt firsthand with the *wages of sin* as clearly stated in John 3:16 and 2 Corinthians 5:19,21. The love of God is a quality of God's nature coequal with his holiness. It was God himself who took the punishment for our sins into his divine being through the human suffering and death of Jesus Christ. The divine love absorbs the divine wrath. The suffering of God in Jesus Christ opened up the doors so that God's love could flow out. The moral lines of the universe are preserved.

An implication of this emphasis as it applies to politics and economics would be that in these arenas compassion takes its place alongside justice. Along with the call to moral accountability and individual responsibility comes an emphasis on suffering with and extending mercy to the last and to the least. The world's view of power is questioned.

*The prophetic role of Christ comes into focus in his Galilean ministry.*—The Gospels extensively record Christ's words and deeds before his crucifixion. The One who freed us from the bondage of sin and guilt at the cross is the One who also liberated us from error and untruth during his ministry in Galilee. In his life, teaching, and healing, Christ gave us a vision of the being and rule of God. Both God's holiness and love were revealed. In his attitudes, behavior, and teaching, Christ embodied mercy for the sinner, justice for the oppressed, compassion for the neighbor in need, love for the enemy, and obedience and joy in relation to God (see Luke 4:18-19).

This prophetic role of the God who was in Christ in Galilee should influence the political, economic, and social views of each Christian. The poor, the prisoners, the blind, and the oppressed should be a focus of concern. There should obviously be an emphasis on justice, compassion for the needy, and love for the enemy.

*The kingly or royal office of Christ comes to focus in Christ's resurrection and ascension.*—Jesus Christ rules now by virtue of his resurrection and ascension. The world is not ultimately in the hands of Satan and the evil forces which seek to thwart God's plan for us. Although the rule of Christ is still hidden (note the evil, sin, and death in the world), Christians, in virtue of the cross and resurrection, know that Satan has been dethroned and Christ is king (Rom. 8:23). Christians can thus confront the conflict with evil with confidence. Biblical faith and classical Christianity have confidence in the *already* of victory, even though it awaits the *not yet* of its completion (Rom. 8:15-18,37-39).

Fortunately, the victory or triumphant view of the atonement is coming back into its own. The sacrificial, substitutionary, propitiatory, and redemptive views of the atonement all have validity. However, the triumphant view must take its proper place. Much of the New Testament has to do with the power of Satan and demons, and this victory view should be seen as quite important.

The death of Christ accomplished the defeat of evil powers. This is clearly set forth in Colossians 2:15. George Ladd, for example, feels that a more satisfactory translation of Colossians 2:15 is that of the Revised Standard Version which understands the verse to mean that Christ has disarmed the evil spiritual powers, stripping them of their insignia of rank or of their arms. Thus the verse states that by his death and resurrection, Christ triumphed over his spiritual enemies, winning a divine victory over the cosmic powers.

The main concern of the Bible is not with the devil but with God and the gospel of his grace. Satan and the demonic have been overcome by the life, death, and resurrection of Jesus Christ. The New Testament never allows complete pessimism. In the end, Satan and his angels will be completely overcome (1 John 3:8).

Evangelicals need to balance the priestly, prophetic, and kingly work of Christ. We must not separate God from the work of Jesus and divine holiness from divine love. Today it is especially important to stress the work of Christ as prophet, king, and priest.

### The Contemporary Christ

We must always seek to bridge the gulf between the world of Jesus and our culture, between Nazareth and Jerusalem and Tokyo and Nairobi. Christ is the Savior and Lord of twentieth-century people, too, and must be presented in terms that are full of meaning for them. But we must beware of the temptation to create our own image of Christ. Attempts have been made to portray him as a liberator, a forerunner of freedom-fighters, and the champion of the oppressed. These portrayals have rightly drawn attention to neglected aspects of the Gospels. But the church's beliefs about Christ will outlive attempts to fit him into contemporary programs. Christ is greater than all these portrayals.[5]

Furthermore, Christianity will not tolerate the view that there are many revelations or various roads to salvation. Nor can it share the view of Hinduism which teaches that since "all roads lead to God" people have to find that road which suits best their nature. In the Christian perspective, God has revealed himself fully and definitively in the person of Jesus Christ and has through his work made available to humankind an all-sufficient redemption.

The truth of creation is indeed reflected in all world religions, but, because of sin and the fall, we believe that we must have a new creation. As Christians, following the New Testament teaching, the saving gospel of reconciliation and redemption is to be found only in Christianity. There are many roads by which people seek to come to God, but there is only one road by which God comes to people in a final and saving way, namely, Jesus Christ.

## Salvation: Restitution, Release, and Renewal

It was revival time in a county seat in Missouri. The children from nine years of age and up had been taught the plan of salvation and had been placed on prayer lists. The evangelist preached on the horrors of being lost now and for eternity. Then he told of God's sending Christ to die for us and to be raised to God's right hand. He told us the Holy Spirit was convicting us. As a ten-year-old boy, I went forward to accept Christ as my personal Savior.

Thirty-seven years later revivals were held in a much more sophisticated church building in Texas. My ten-year-old son attended. I was elsewhere. When I returned home, he was waiting—under conviction of sin. The next night he went forward to make a public profession of his personal faith in Jesus Christ.

I fell away from active church life in college days. This is sometimes called backsliding. But at a youth revival, I rededicated my life to Jesus and knew a renewal and revitalizing of my Christian life.

The above descriptions indicate the way salvation begins and continues for many evangelical Christians.

To see salvation in a broad sense it must be affirmed that we have been saved, we are being saved, and we shall be saved. In the section on the person and work of Christ, we saw that the historical basis of salvation was provided by the saving events that took place in Jesus Christ and the coming of the Holy Spirit. In the section on last things, we will look at the end point of the process of salvation. In this section, we will look at how our salvation reaches us in the present in grace and is personally received by us in faith. This is the *subjective* side of the salvation process which is the application of the benefits of salvation provided in the work of Christ.

Salvation *now* is the gracious work of the Holy Spirit in bringing Christ and all his benefits to us today. In the doctrine of personal salvation, the order is seen as calling, regeneration, conversion (repentance and faith), justification, sanctification, perseverance, and glorification. An individual called by God to be among the saved is born again. He or she experiences "new being" in personal repentance and faith, stands pardoned before God, grows in personal holiness, avoids the temptations of backsliding, and receives the blessings of heaven in the world to come. The entire pilgrimage is carried out by God's grace, not by human works. Christ delivers us from sin and death.

### Salvation from Sin

*Justification by faith.*—In the New Testament, many metaphors are used to express the reality of Christian salvation. One metaphor, used primarily by Paul, is "justification by faith" (Rom. 3:28; Gal. 3:11).

*Justification* is a term borrowed from the law courts of the first century. The judge heard an accusation against a person and declared the accused "justified." "Not guilty" or "innocent" were simply not strong enough words to express what the judge meant. He was really saying, "You stand before this court as one who is in the right" (Gal. 3:13).

It is important to realize, therefore, that justification is not primarily a statement of a person's moral worth. It is about a person being legally in the right. When used in a Christian sense, justification by faith is a statement about our standing before God. It does not declare that we *are* righteous but that in God's sight we are in a right relationship with him (2 Cor. 5:21).

We need to be justified because we are in a serious position before God. We are incapable of rescuing ourselves. Salvation is only possible if it comes from God (Rom. 3:23-24).

When God justifies me, he does not look at my qualities but at the qualities of Jesus Christ. We are made right by his righteousness, not our own (1 Cor. 1:30; 2 Cor. 5:21). We can contribute nothing to our salvation except a willingness to respond—to reach out toward the Christian life, to take it, and live it in the power of the Spirit.

We know that we deserve a guilty verdict, but the Christian gospel states that in Jesus Christ we are set unreservedly free. We are filled with gratitude for the generosity we have been shown and are amazed at such love (Rom 12:1). A new life now begins—new life made possible through the Holy Spirit given to all who follow Jesus.

Justification is a glorious doctrine. It takes us to the heart of the good news and is at the center of Christian preaching. Ignore its truth and Christianity stands in danger of confusion and heresy.[6]

*Faith as assent and trust.*—Faith is assent (surrender) to the biblical statement of who God is and what Christ does. But this faith is trust at the deepest level as well as belief. Faith is a crucial decision, not something casually assumed. Especially in Paul's letters and in John's Gospel, we find that faith means trusting our whole life to God. The modern word *commitment* comes very close to this. What is required is not just assent to an idea but humble acceptance of what God has done. Faith, then, is trust in what God has done, which results in a wholehearted commitment, trusting ourselves to him. This affects every area of our lives.

The Bible also makes it clear that faith cannot be separated from our lives, our behavior, and the world we live in. James wrote that "faith by itself, if it has no works, is dead" (2:17). But he was not contradicting the emphasis in the rest of the New Testament that we are saved by faith alone. His point was that mere intellectual belief is barren. The demons believe in God, he said, but it makes no difference to their conduct (2:19). A real faith will always issue in a changed life.

In summary, to have faith is to accept what God has revealed of himself in Jesus. To have faith is to yield ourselves to Jesus in the light of what he has revealed.

*Conversion.*—*Born again* or *from above* or *anew* or *conversion* are terms used to describe that unique experience in which an individual is united with God in Christ and is made into a "new creature" (John 3:3; 2 Cor. 5:17). From the human side, conversion involves repentance, faith, and confession (Rom. 3:9-10). From the divine side, it involves forgiveness grounded in the death of Christ, regeneration through the agency of the Holy Spirit, justification, and adoption (Rom. 5:1-2). This conversion experience happens only once.

Most Evangelicals see authentic conversion as revolutionary and not evolutionary. Repentance and faith take hold in an instantaneous and dramatic way. Regeneration is seen as the intense personal experience given as a sign of one's new relationship to God and not merely a status conferred in baptism (2 Cor. 5:17-18).

Conversion, or turning, always involves at least three factors. First, there is awareness of need. No one comes to faith in Jesus without a sense that something is missing in life. This can take different forms with different people. One person may be conscious of moral failure or an inability to overcome temptation. Another may be aware of a sense of frustration and futility of life. Another may come to realize that life has no meaning unless God is brought into the picture. Mary Magdalene, Paul, and Peter had different experiences.

Second, there is a willingness to turn. The word for this is *repentance.* The word for *repentance* in Greek means to turn around or have a change of heart and attitude. Repentance involves being sincerely sorry for our sin and willing to change direction (Acts 3:19; 2 Cor. 7:10).

Third, there is faith in Jesus Christ. Turning is one thing but in itself is not enough. Many people like to turn over a new leaf, but this does not make them Christians.

Jesus called people to repent and believe the gospel (Mark 1:15). A person must accept Jesus as who he claimed to be, the Savior and Lord of his life. By a conscious decision, I turn my back on my old life and enter a new life based on Jesus. I become a disciple, a follower of Jesus, who learns his way.

If Jesus died for sinners and rose to prove it, the Christian must die to the old nature and begin afresh through the Holy Spirit. This is expressed symbolically in baptism. Indeed, baptism in the New Testament and in the early church was in itself a symbol of conversion. It graphically declared a person's rejection of the old life and entry into new life through the Holy Spirit (Rom. 6:3-4).

For some, conversion is a crisis event. But the experience of other Christians in all traditions of the Christian church is that this discovery of faith may come without any major outward crisis or easily identifiable turning point. And yet it remains true that awareness of need, willingness to turn, and belief in Jesus are essential to Christianity itself. A person who has them all is a converted person.

Following our emphasis on covenant, conversion, as it is understood in the Bible, is an act of *entering into convenant* with a new covenant partner, Almighty God. This means coming under a new set of demands. It also means entering into a different history, embracing a different memory, and living with different promises. And from that, of course, comes a new perception on the world and a new life-style. Life is seen and understood in new ways and one lives, in response, in a very different way (Gal. 4:24-30; Rom. 12:1-2).[7]

*Grace as sanctification.*—Sanctification is included under the general category of salvation. Traditional evangelical theology has thought of justification, regeneration, and adoption as the beginning of the Christian life and sanctification as the progressive unfolding of that life. Sanctification, however, can be described from several perspectives.

In one sense, every Christian has the Holy Spirit and is a saint (1 Cor. 1:2). From this perspective, sanctification is a work of God. In this sense, sanctification embraces all of God's actions and is equivalent to justification. "But you were sanctified, you were justified in the name of the Lord Jesus Christ and in the Spirit of our God" (1 Cor. 6:11). The whole of Christian existence, as such, is the work of the Holy Spirit and, as such, is sanctification. In fact, the New Testament is insistent that no one is a Christian unless he is indwelt by the Holy Spirit (Rom. 8:9). Every believer is sealed in the Spirit and is thus given assurance that his salvation will be fulfilled in the "age to come" (2 Cor. 1:22).

On the other hand, every Christian needs the Holy Spirit and is *progressively* to become what he is in vital principle. In addition to the broad concept of sanctification as being completely the work of God, the Bible has a more narrow concept, which distinguishes sanctification from justification. From the narrow perspective, sanctification is not thought of as the unique event which brings into reality the new creature. Rather, it refers to the processes of growth through which a sinful person develops into a more godly person. From this view, sanctification is the gradual growth of the new person as he goes forward under the progressive influence of the Holy Spirit.

Although, from the broad perspective, the Christian is already sanctified, he is to become sanctified (1 Thess. 5:23). This attempt to appropriate the Spirit's work is a difficult (from a human perspective) and never-ending spiritual struggle. Tension is created. On the one hand, the Christian is a person who all at once is indwelt by the Holy Spirit and reconciled. On the other hand, he has yet to become what he already is through the acquittal of justifying grace. But once again it must be said that the "once-for-allness" of justification is basic and the beginning point. The Christian believes that by faith, in the center of his being, he is already a new creature. However, in experience, he has not yet attained that character. He must actually become what God already sees him to be. To that end, Evangelicals insist on regular worship, devotional Bible study, prayer, and retreats. There must not be such a fixation on the initial experience of conversion that growing up into spiritual adulthood is ignored.

Evangelicals try to remind themselves, however, that the Christian's inner life in Christ is and must be energized by the Spirit. This sanctification or restoration of what belongs to God can happen only through the help of his power. But adrift from the Spirit's power, sanctification becomes legalistic moralism and humanly impossible.

The advance in sanctification often comes through growth crises. Christian sanctification can be seen as a series of forward thrusts by God into man's sinful nature.

Sanctification can be approached from still another perspective. The Christian's ethical goal is the fruit of the Spirit which is Christlikeness (Gal. 5:22-23). The supreme gift of the Spirit is to live for others (1 Cor. 12:31 to 13:13). Because the new age has come, the Christian experiences spiritual growth, ethical victory, and usage of gifts. The New Testament concept of sanctification does not mean world denial but service to God and neighbor.

Christ's purpose is not to suppress our humanity and turn us into world-denying ascetics or religious fanatics. He plans to make us into people as whole as he was, rightly related to God and one another in every aspect of our personalities, bodies, thoughts, emotions, and actions. He wants us to have a proper concern for and involvement in every aspect of the life of this world that God created and wants to redeem.

Christian holiness is positive and human, not negative and joyless. If it often involves self-denial, that is only a means to the promotion of Jesus' new humanity in us and in others, so that we may have the abundant life (see John 10:10).

Every Christian awaits the final perfecting work of the Spirit. All teaching on sanctification stands under the sign of the second coming and the "Age to Come." Christians realize their incompleteness in this age. The Christian now has only the "first fruits" or "earnest" of the Spirit (2 Cor. 1:22; Eph. 1:14, KJV). The "New Age" is till the "Age to Come." Christians must not affirm that they have arrived.

The Spirit, although future in its fullness, already is releasing a dynamic and transforming power. Awaiting total fulfillment, the Christian is sealed with this Holy Spirit (2 Cor. 1:21-22; Eph. 1:13-14). It is important to keep the balance of New Testament teaching about sanctification and avoid extremes. We must not fall into a *pessimism* which limits our expectation of the real changes that God is able to make at every stage of our life. We can never say, "I am as I am; I shall never change now." That is to close ourselves to the sanctifying power of the Spirit to break old habits and pour the transforming love of God into our hearts.

We need to avoid an unrealistic *optimism* which sees perfect sanctification as something easily and quickly within our grasp. The battle against sin is lifelong and continual. When we have conquered it on one level (such as the physical sins), it breaks out again on another (such as the spiritual sins). We shall never be done with sin or know final and complete victory over it this side of heaven.

Thus we see that personal salvation is also *power over* as well as *pardon* of sin. Despite all the pitfalls of pride and self-righteousness, God makes people whole as well as declaring them forgiven (Rom. 6:12-14). Fruit of love can be seen. Sanctification is a stage of real growth in holiness. Perfectionist impulses often obscure the sin that persists in the life of the redeemed. Along with growth there must be a place for continuing penitence and self-criticism even for prominent Christian leaders.

Social sanctification also calls for self-criticism and penitence in regard to the wrong type of superpatriotism, the oversimplification of Christian politicians, and dogmatic Christian social positions. The give-to-get motif of the appeals of some television preachers reminds one of the selling of indulgences in the time of Martin Luther. We must remember that salvation cannot be bought.

Some televangelists also tend to shape the way the Christian message is presented to the style of television commercials. For some, slogans and quick-fix promises tend to replace the richness and subtlety of Christian faith and detour around the strenuous road of Christian sanctification.

In his earthly ministry, Christ liberated enslaved people. The living and contemporary Christ is in our midst still liberating people. Through grace we are delivered from evil and called to enter into the healing stream where Christ is at work in the world. Liberation theology has increased our awareness of the presence of organized evil and the importance of contesting it. Christ is also working in social areas to heal and deliver.

### Salvation from Death

A great fire raged. The flames reached the third floor. A gray-haired fireman climbed up the towering ladder and reached into a window of the third story where the streams of water were hissing against the flames to rescue a child. He held the child secure in his arms and with sure grip climbed down the ladder to safety. The child looked fearfully about but still rested securely in the arms of the rescuer.

And so it is with us if we are in Christ. We are not spared physical death. We will see the flames through which we are being carried. The streams of water will hiss about us. But we have One in whose arms we may rest. We have Christ who will bear us safely through fire and water to the safety of eternal life (John 3:36).

The death that is the "wages of sin" is, in the deepest sense, separation from God. In its broadest sense, it is alienation. The freedom based on Christ's death and resurrection frees us from the alienation from God. We are given *now* in an anticipatory way the fellowship with God, humanity, and nature which will be our final destiny. We are opened to new possibilities and given new hope. Despair paralyzes but hope mobilizes. The final conquest comes with the return of Christ (1 Cor. 15:20-24). But the "sting of death" is taken away. The risen Christ is the Lord of the future. With faith in Christ, we have hope for the future opened to us.

### Notes

1. Gabriel Fackre, *The Christian Story* (Grand Rapids, MI: Wm. B. Eerdmans, 1978), p. 81.

2. Gabriel Fackre, *The Religious Right and Christian Faith* (Grand Rapids, MI: Wm. B. Eerdmans, 1982), p. 62.

3. Robin Keeley, ed., *Eerdmans' Handbook to Christian Belief* (Grand Rapids, MI: Wm. B. Eerdmans, 1982), p. 108.

4. Donald G. Bloesch, *Essentials of Evangelical Theology,* Vol. 2: *Life, Ministry, and Hope* (San Francisco: Harper & Row, 1979), p. 248.

5. Keeley, p. 80.

6. Keeley, pp. 344-346.

7. Walter Brueggemann, *The Bible Makes Sense* (Atlanta: John Knox Press, 1977), pp. 93-94.

### Bibliography

Achtemeier, Paul J. and Elizabeth. *The Old Testament Roots of Our Faith.* Nashville: Abingdon Press, 1962.

Bloesch, Donald G. *Essentials of Evangelical Theology.* Vol. 2: *Life, Ministry, & Hope.* San Francisco: Harper & Row, 1979.

Brueggemann, Walter. *The Bible Makes Sense.* Atlanta: John Knox Press, 1977.

Fackre, Gabriel. *The Christian Story.* Grand Rapids: Eerdmans, 1978.

_____. *The Religious Right and Christian Faith.* Grand Rapids, MI: Wm. B. Eerdmans, 1982.

Keeley, Robin, ed. *Eerdmans' Handbook to Christian Belief.* Grand Rapids, MI: Wm. B. Eerdmans, 1982.

Newport, John P. "The Theology and Experience of Salvation." *The Greek Orthodox Theological Review,* Vol. XXII, No. 4 (Winter 1977): 393-404

# 8
# The Church and the Doctrine of Last Things

## The Church: God's Redemptive Instrument

On the very day that I was writing this section, I had fellowship with two pastors. One was from an Eastern European country behind the Iron Curtain. The other was from Australia. Both were excited about what God was doing through their particular churches on opposite sides of the world. What is the church? What are its marks, its mission, its nature, and its ministries?

### Ascension and Pentecost (Bridge from Christ to the Church)

After the ascension of Christ which declared his glorified humanity, the truly human, truly divine, truly one Jesus is now the world's Lord. This ascent of the Son was followed by the descent of the Holy Spirit (the Spirit had already been working before his coming at Pentecost). On Pentecost, the Holy Spirit brought to be in a more formal way the body of Christ on earth. The few hundred new Christians found that they had been made a living community through Jesus' resurrection and the Holy Spirit's outpouring at Pentecost. Something new and dynamic was happening. Both believers and nonbelievers sensed the unusual stirring and the feeling of a new movement being born (Acts 2:41).

And yet, as with all God's work in history, the Spirit's new work was related to his work in earlier days. The new Christian community had roots in the Old Testament and in God's ancient chosen people, Israel. Even Peter on the Day of Pentecost made the connection with God's work in the past, "This is what was spoken by the prophet Joel" (Acts 2:16). King David himself, Peter said, was Jesus' forerunner and looked ahead to the New Israel (Acts 2:25-26).

Jumping across twenty centuries to today's world is not impossible or strange, for it is the same Spirit of Jesus who works in the church today. As with the believers at Pentecost, so today the church is at root the community of people who confess Jesus as Lord and commit themselves to live for God's kingdom.

The New Testament describes the birth of the Christian community. It gives enough information and insight for believers to understand how the church is to function. God intends his disciples to be guided by both the Spirit and his written Word, as they carry on church life today. It should be remembered that the Holy Spirit, who inspired the writers of the New Testament, will not lead us to violate the principles of the New Testament.

When Paul and his missionary group set out from Antioch, they planted new church communities throughout much of the Mediterranean world. We learn of these new communities in Paul's letters as well as in Acts.

The New Testament writings show that at the basic level of truth, principle, and spiritual dynamic these communities were quite similar. But at the level of custom and culture, they displayed variations. In each case, the church was the body of Christ, the New Israel, and the community of God's people.

It is important for the church today to constantly return to the New Testament for its guidelines. For example, the growing split between clergy and laity, with all authentic witness and authority pretty well reserved for male clergy in some churches, tends to reduce the church's vitality to less than the New Testament dynamic.

The Spirit's vital work in history has been to re-create and restore the church as a living community, calling it back to its biblical life and roots. We must constantly seek to return the churches to the New Testament pattern of organization and to the power of the Spirit in each generation.[1]

### The Marks of the Church

The early church proclaimed the gospel, continued in worship, served neighbors in need, and shared a remarkable fellowship. In addition to the *proclamation* of the gospel and *worship,* the early church was characterized by at least three marks.

*First, fellowship and community.*—In the biblical picture of the church, fellowship and community are as vitally important as worship (Acts 2:44-47). According to the Bible, community and fellowship mean shared life together, based on our new being in Jesus Christ. To be born again is to be born into God's family and community. Any group of believers which fails to experience intimate life together has failed to experience the church as Christ's living body.

*Second, discipline.*—The church is not a chance collection of people, but a community of believers called and united together by the grace of God—a covenant people. Christian believers, therefore, accept responsibility for each other and agree to exercise such discipline as is necessary to remain faithful to God's covenant (1 Cor. 5:1-5). The church takes seriously the Bible's instructions to warn, rebuke, exhort, encourage, and build one another up in love.

*Third, service.*—The early church took responsibility for the welfare of Christian brothers and sisters in their social, material, and spiritual needs (Acts 2:45).

### The Mission of the Church

The mission of the church grew out of the mission of God. This mission involved deeds, proclamation, evangelistic call, and prophetic confrontation. Church and mission are inseparable. There is no church without mission nor mission without the church. The agent of mission is the Holy Spirit, but the Holy Spirit works through the church.

In a healthy Christian community, witness springs not only from Jesus' specific commission but also from the power of the Holy Spirit and the dynamic of Christian community life. A living Christian community has both the desire and the power to witness. Witness is the inevitable and necessary fruit of a worshiping, nurturing community and is the highest priority of the church's life in the world (Acts 2:47).

The church's witness includes evangelism and service. Both are basic forms of Christian witness. Each strengthens and reinforces the other. Where the church's evangelistic witness has been undergirded by loving service in the spirit of Jesus and where service has been joined with evangelism, there the church has been at its best by word and by deed.[2]

This does not mean that all Christians are meant to be evangelists with a special formal calling to proclaim the gospel to those who have not yet received it. But all Christians are meant to be witnesses: people whose words, relationships, attitudes, and abilities point beyond themselves to the living Lord who is the source of all their lives.

The church is fully the church when it sees the vision and hears God's

Word and then goes into the world to be God's instrument of redemption. This mission is not only to give personal witness and reflect personal morality but also to struggle for peace, justice, freedom, and respect for the environment (Matt. 25:34-46). Christians are now becoming more sensitive to the biblical teachings which call for concern for the poor, the hungry, the Third-World countries, women, elderly citizens, and the disabled.

But an order of priority must be established. As we noted in the chapter on the "The Guiding Key," Jesus related the preaching of the gospel to the end of the world and to his return (Matt. 24:14). This means that evangelism and the planting of new churches must be the primary mission of a New Testament church. This would obviously involve a genuine global partnership among Christians in all six continents.

### The Nature of the Church

The church is called to radical obedience to God's will. Such an obedience results in a gathered or committed church. Some would divide the church into two basic concepts: the "church-type" and the "gathered-church-type."

*The "church-type" is more inclusive and lets the wheat and tares grow together (Matt. 13:30).*—In more theological terms, the "church-type" views the holiness of the church as a new redeemed position or status conferred by the Spirit, through the sacraments, on a company of sinners. It does not see the qualifications for church membership as a certain state of moral and spiritual experience and attainment which can be outwardly demonstrated.

The *"gathered-church" concept* calls for explicit or open evidences of a spiritual experience with Christ or a born-again condition. Despite its emphasis on a personal and saving experience with Christ and high standards for church membership, the "gathered" or "committed" church realizes that it is not perfect. It sees itself as a community of the future which now lives under the conditions of the present age. The church is called out of the present and toward the future, but it sees that it is not yet living in that future. The Spirit is present and so new life is present although the church stands in constant need of renewal.

Renewals, or awakenings, have been a key feature of Christian history. Without them the church would have become increasingly lifeless and would have lacked what we now see as its essential characteristics.

Renewal leaders are still sinners and are in constant danger of pride and self-righteousness. But they are needed as critics-in-residence and as potential instruments of God's Spirit.

### The Ministries of the Church

*General Ministry*—The church lives by the Holy Spirit. The Spirit gives the church the gifts of proclamation, service, fellowship, and worship. In one sense, when one dies to the old life and is baptized, one is ordained to the general ministry of the church. This general concept of ministry does not distinguish between clergy and laity but speaks of all believers as constituting the people or laity of God. Peter wrote that the church is "a chosen people, a royal priesthood, a holy nation, God's own people" (1 Pet. 2:9) for the purpose of declaring God's glory.

Through Christ's priestly work, all believers are made God's priests. This means that all believers have direct access to God. It also means that Christians are priests to each other. Believers serve and minister to each other and in the world as part of the universal priesthood.

*Gifts and fruit of the Spirit.*—Another aspect of the universal ministry of the church is related to the gifts of the Spirit. Paul made it clear that believers have different gifts according to the grace given them. Every believer is to seek to manifest all the fruit of the Spirit. But with the gifts of the Spirit, the point is diversity; the gifts vary. The point is that every gift is a functional gift and is to be used to serve others and to glorify God. Christians exercise their priestly ministry in part through the gifts God gives (1 Cor. 12:4-7).

Two things can be said about spiritual gifts. One, every believer has some spiritual gift. Gifts are not restricted to leaders but are given to all Christians. To be a Christian means to be part of Christ's body, and every part of the body has some function (1 Cor. 12:12-25). Second, genuine Christian ministry is first and foremost the gracious ministry of God's Spirit through our personalities. It is at root a matter of God's grace, not of human ability. Christian ministry is carried out by more than human efforts, so it produces more than human results (1 Cor. 2:1-5).

At this point, it should be noted that the gifts of the Spirit to us must not be confused with the fruit of the Spirit within us. We are given gifts of the Spirit so that we can more effectively serve. But if we become preoccupied with the gifts by which we serve, and thus neglect the people we are called to love, we pervert the work the Spirit has given us. The fruit of the Spirit is "love, joy, peace, patience, kindness, goodness, faithfulness, gentleness, self-control" (Gal. 5:22-23). These are the marks of a mature Christian. Without this fruit with a chief emphasis on love, our spiritual gifts are nothing—they are of no use to us or to the fellowship of Christians (1 Cor. 13:1-3).[3]

*Types of gifts.*—The gifts of the Spirit for the preservation and vigorous life of the church can be identified as of two types. One type of gifts assures the identity of the church and is the vehicle of the continuation of the ministry of the church. The other type of gifts guarantees the true vitality of the church and is the organ of its hope.

The first type of gifts includes people who are called to a special ministry which primarily involves spiritual oversight, proclamation, and worship leadership (1 Cor. 3:5; 2 Tim. 1:11). The principal duties are to assure the identity and continuation of the ministry of the church. This type of gift emphasizes preaching of the Word and the administration of the ordinances, and spiritual leadership. This is a particular ministry with its distinctive functions usually designated by ordination.

The "gathered-church" approach seeks to follow the New Testament pattern in its development of this aspect of ministry.

> The most significant officer in the New Testament as connected with a local church was that of pastor. There are three terms used in the New Testament for that office—pastor, elder, and bishop. In Acts 20, in the account of Paul's meeting with the elders of the church at Ephesus, in verse 17, they are called "elders," while in verse 28 Paul calls them "bishops" (AS). The verb translated "feed" in verse 28 means to tend as a shepherd, act as shepherd. This is the verb corresponding to the noun that is translated "pastor." So here in one passage, the same men are called "elders" and "bishops" and they are exhorted to "pastor" the flock. Again, in Titus 1: 5, 7, Paul uses the terms "elders" and "bishops" to apply to the same office. In 1 Peter 5: 1, 2, Peter addresses the "elders," and exhorts them to "pastor" or "shepherd" the flock.
>
> The duties of the pastors are not defined in detail in the New Testament. Evidently they were intended to exercise general oversight in spiritual matters, teach their people, and guide in all the activities of the church. Their character and spiritual attainments must be such as to qualify them for such leadership (1 Tim. 3: 1ff.; Titus 1: 5ff.; 1 Peter 5: 1ff.).[4]

The Catholic approach concentrates on priestly and sacramental ministry in which the priest is set apart to represent the flock. However, the

Protestant approach concentrates on the ministry of the Word, in preaching and pastoral care. It is a more functional approach to ordination.

Both the right and left wings of the Protestant Reformation would have difficulty with the vesting of nearly absolute power in the person and office of the pastor. There developed in the Reformation an awareness of the temptations of power and the tendency toward spiritual pride. In the left-wing Reformation tradition, there was opposition to the bishops and kings and an insistence on the dispersion of power among the members of the churches. They saw the Spirit as spread throughout the membership of the whole body giving a variety of gifts rather than just being concentrated in the person of the pastor. The pastor was seen as more of an equipper, enabler, and general overseer.

The second type of gifts includes those who are called to emphasize the gifts of vitality including service and fellowship (deacons). These are laypersons who are called to the upbuilding and outreaching in love of the body of Christ (Rom. 12:4-8; 1 Cor. 12:27-31; Eph. 4:11-12).

The gathered church finds in the New Testament another class of leaders different from the pastor. The choosing of the seven in Acts 6:1-6 is sometimes considered as the origin of the office of deacon. The seven were not called deacons in that chapter, however, and there is no positive proof that this was the origin of that office. As a functional group or class of officers, deacons are first named in Philippians 1:1.

The qualifications of deacons were to be much the same as those of pastors or bishops (1 Tim. 3:8-10,12-13). Not much is said to throw light on their duties or functions.Their qualifications, however, indicate that they were to perform their duties for spiritual purposes or ends.

While pastors and deacons are the only officers of a local church clearly referred to in the New Testament, we cannot be sure that the churches had no others. The commission given to us to spread the gospel and to develop churches justifies us in using any means or adopting any methods that are consistent with the principles of the gospel and the fundamentals of New Testament church life. For example, the principles of the New Testament are congenial with the democratic organization of the church and a multiple church ministry.

The ministry of the laity is also in the foreground of the mission of the church in places of work and leisure. In some cases, there is a formal commissioning or consecrating of laity to this ministry. As we have noted, this is especially done in the ordination of laity to the office of deacon. In some cases, the service of the deacon is confined to the inreach aspect of the church and oftentimes trivialized in even that limited area. The churches flowing from the left wing of the Reformation would place more emphasis on lay leadership in all areas of church life.

In any case, this emphasis on different responsibilities should not be hardened into a rigid division of ministry. The clergy must surely emphasize and in some way participate in all phases of ministry. The clergy are responsible for proclamation and worship and general spiritual leadership but do not have a monopoly on them. The laity, both men and women, must also emphasize proclamation, depth in worship, and deeper spirituality.

### The Worship and the Ordinances of the Church

*Worship.* —The glory, the shekinah of God, is no longer to be found in the Temple. But as John 1:1-4 proclaims, this divine glory has now appeared in the incarnate Word, Jesus Christ. Since Christ—not the Temple—is the center of all worship, it is no longer geographically limited, but all worship becomes worship in the Spirit (John 2:14-21; 4:23-24).

Let us note the relation of the Spirit to worship. In the first place, the Holy Spirit guides worship. In Acts, the Holy Spirit made worship vital and effective for life. There was emotion in New Testament worship, but it was under the control of the historic faith and was not the frenzy of the pagans (1 Cor. 14:40). The New Testament indicates that the early church displayed more emotion in worship than the average evangelical church today. For many this is a contemporary weakness of our churches.

Despite excesses, spiritual worship in the early church was primary. The New Testament church was, first of all, a worshiping fellowship of believers. Worship was not fixed in form. Rather, variety, spontaneity, and freedom characterized the worship. The spirit of worship was reverent response to God's acts and gifts—not a groping quest for God, which marks some modern thought. The spirit of response was gratitude, joy, expectation, and hope.

In the second place, there is no magical note about this worship. The ordinances could not save. The spiritual and moral had precedence over form and ritual. Insincere worship was seen as a damaging thing (1 Cor. 11:29).

Public worship was more like the Jewish synagogue worship than the Jewish Temple worship. Freedom was exerted. Yet the usual features reflect the synagogue pattern. The Scriptures were continually used. Preaching and teaching took different forms according to the situation. Evangelistic preaching was for those outside and explanation of meaning was provided for believers. Psalms and, later, Christian hymns and songs were used. The use of spiritual songs indicates the difference between Christian and pagan hymns (Eph. 5:19). The hymns were not generalized religious sentimentalism. They expressed in clear-cut statements, praise for the saving activity of God in Christ. They often had the character of confessions of faith. Moffatt says that more than a score of hymns are quoted in part or in whole in 1 Corinthians alone.

Prayer was central with an emphasis upon thanksgiving for God's gracious gifts. The ordinances symbolized God's gift and moved the people to gratitude and response and dedication. There were no magical blessings or automatic gifts or priestly control. There was an offering upon the first day of the week (1 Cor. 16:2).

The aim of the worship service was to build up the Christian community. There was freedom in the service and yet order. A restudy of New Testament worship reveals that free worship and a more ordered worship are not mutually exclusive alternatives. This means that what is most orderly and faithful to the gospel is also most free and open. Evangelical Christians are concerned to provide an ordered framework within which the freedom of the Spirit can most effectively operate.

*Baptism and the Lord's Supper.*—From the beginning, the identity of the New Testament church was sharpened by the central events of baptism and the Lord's Supper. These ordinances constitute the sign language of Christianity. Guidelines as to matter or external content and the form of administration are given in the New Testament. There are other subordinate acts which strengthen the church and the pilgrimage of faith, such as marriage, ordination, confession, and counsel—public and private. There is also burial at the end of the journey. But the central focus is on the two ordinances rising out of the ministry and example and commission of Christ.

When the water is joined to the baptismal word in the act of baptism, there is symbolized a spiritual burial and rising again (Rom. 6:3-5).

Baptism can also act as a confession, and it portrays a new environment and a new relationship. The person baptized is called by Jesus Christ to be a participant in the ongoing drama of redemption.

Problems arising from the practice of infant or household baptism, especially in the lands where there is a state church, have led the great Protestant theologians, Karl Barth and Jurgen Moltmann to favor believer's baptism. When Moltmann's book *The Church in the Power of the Spirit* was translated into English, *Time* magazine stated that in one aspect of doctrine Moltmann had come to a radical conclusion for a theologian nurtured in a state church. Moltmann argues that infant baptism should be phased out because it signifies ties to "family, nation, and society" as much as a person's identification with Christ. The church, Moltmann says, should baptize only those who are able to "confess their faith."

Those who hold believers baptism make a number of emphases. First, it is insisted that the New Testament teaches that the subject of baptism must be a believer in the gospel of Christ. This excludes infant and household baptism, preserves the personal meaning of Christianity, and emphasizes the spiritual nature of the church.

In the second place, it is insisted that the New Testament teaches that the mode or form must be immersion. The outward act is not as important as its spiritual conditions, but it is still important because the New Testament commands it and because the symbolism of death-resurrection calls for immersion.

In the third place, this view affirms that the New Testament has some definite teachings about the significance of baptism. In reference to Christ, it is an act of obedience to Christ, it is a confession of faith, it is a profession of conversion, and it is a dedication of life to union with Christ in his death and resurrection. Most people who hold believer's baptism state that baptism in itself is symbolic and does not convey grace or salvation.

In recent years, there has been a growing stress upon the decisiveness of confirmation where household or infant baptism is practiced. Confirmation is seen as a recognition of the importance of the personal act of faith at the age of personal accountability. In turn, the rite of "dedication" of children (in reality, the dedication of parents and the church to Christian nurture and witness) is widely observed in denominations which stress believer's baptism.

Following the initial ordinance of baptism, the New Testament church celebrated the ordinance of the Lord's Supper. Regrettably, there is widespread disagreement about the meaning and practice of the Lord's Supper. These differences are reflected in the different terms used. Protestants usually speak of the Lord's Supper, the Lord's table, the Holy Communion, or the breaking of bread. Catholics speak of the altar, the Eucharist (a term the Eastern Orthodox also use) or the Mass.

*Eucharist* comes from a Greek word meaning "thanksgiving," and the Mass from the Latin words the priest speaks at the end of the service, *missa est,* indicating that the congregation is dismissed. The Lord's Supper and baptism are usually referred to as sacraments. The Roman Catholic and Eastern Orthodox Churches also include other rites as sacraments, such as marriage and confirmation. The main differences, however, are over the meaning of the Lord's Supper, or more specifically, what happens to the bread and wine and what happens to the worshipers.

The Roman Catholic doctrine of transubstantiation was officially stated in AD 1215 at the Fourth Lateran Council, affirmed and expounded more fully during the sixteenth-century Council of Trent, and reaffirmed in 1965 following the Second Vatican Council. It states that when the priest pronounces the words of Christ, "This is my body" and "This is my blood," the elements of bread and wine are miraculously changed into the body and blood of Jesus. These are then offered to God as an atoning and effective sacrifice for the sins of the living and the dead. It is further stated that, when the congregation partakes of the bread, they really receive Jesus Christ's body and blood.

The Lutheran view, often referred to as consubstantiation, affirms that the glorified human nature of Jesus is really present "in, with, and under" the bread and wine.

The Zwinglian view held by most left-wing Reformation groups (including Baptists and other denominations) stresses that the bread and wine are symbols only. This view concentrates on the remembrance aspect of the meal (1 Cor. 11:24-25). Most people who hold the symbolic view consider the Lord's Supper a church ordinance and not an individual obligation or means of grace. Thus, according to the symbolic view, the Lord's Supper is observed only at a public service of the local church and is not served to individuals in the home or at conventions. This view realizes that it may be impressive at a convention but affirms that it is not the Lord's Supper in the strict New Testament sense. Since it is a memorial service and not primarily an act of worship, this view holds that the Lord's Supper need not be repeated with every occasion of worship. Rather, the Lord's Supper should be observed often enough to prevent an attitude of neglect but not so often as to become a matter of mere routine. In the New Testament, there is no closed or open communion, for the Lord's Supper is for those in the church fellowship.

The Calvinist view was formed by John Calvin when he tried to mediate between Luther and Zwingli who disagreed strongly over these matters. Calvin taught that Jesus is really present when the bread is eaten and the wine drunk, but present in a spiritual way.

For Evangelicals, the Lord's Supper is rich in significance and should be observed regularly with reverence. In the observance, we look back to the cross with grief for our sin and gratitude for our salvation. We look up to an exalted Savior, present with us by his Spirit, offering again to our faith the rich experience of his fellowship, his forgiveness, and his strength.

When the Spirit is at work in the Lord's Supper service, it cannot remain just a memorial service looking back to his sacrifice long ago. It becomes instead a celebration of the presence of the Lord. Once crucified, he is now risen and comes to share his new life with us and to enable us to share it with one another and others.

We look around to our brothers and sisters in the family of Christ and rejoice that God has made us his community. We also look forward with longing and anticipation to what the Book of Revelation calls "the marriage supper of the Lamb" (19:9) for we celebrate the supper on earth "until he comes" (1 Cor. 11:26).[5]

### Conclusion

God has formed his people into a community, body, and household. The church is called to be in the world yet not of the world. It can only respond to this call if it is truly distinct, living as God's counterculture.

In fact, however, the church through history has frequently failed to embody the reality of the kingdom in its life and witness. Yet precisely at such times God has often renewed his church, calling it back to its New Testament basis and its true purpose.

Today increasing numbers of Christian believers are becoming sensitive to the biblical marks of the church. In fact, believers on all continents appear to be recovering the living dynamic of the church as the community of God's people following the New Testament pattern.

## Last Things: The Fulfillment and the Life Beyond

### The Importance of Last Things

*From a more general perspective, we can say that there is a widespread sense of the need for a doctrine of last things in our time.*—Scientific knowledge and technical skills continue to increase. Despite increased knowledge we live in a fear-haunted world. The voice of philosophy is strangely silent in regard to ultimate questions. Such answers as it gives to our questions are mainly negative.

When more normative Christian groups do not speak out clearly on last things, many turn to the sects and cults which are increasingly active. Although their teachings have little basis in historical reality, they thrive on promises of a secret glimpse into the future.

This loss of Christian hope in our time has brought inevitable consequences. For example, for many there is a panic fear of the end. Without an adequate hope, many people are scrambling for material goods and pleasure. Television commercials urge us to live with gusto because we only go around once.

*From a more personal perspective, there are reasons why we need to consider the doctrine of last things.*—All of us face death and the end of our own lives in spite of the advances of medical science. If you have no hope, you will lose meaning and perspective in life.

But down deep, most people want to know about last things and want to live on beyond death in a fulfilled life. We also want to believe our loved ones live on beyond death. Recently I visited my family home and looked again at pictures of my father who has been dead for several years. I remembered the wonderful fellowship which we had. For almost twenty-five years, he wrote me a letter or postcard every week. I long to see him again.

### Inadequate Views of Last Things

There are many less than personal views of last things and immortality that are presented to the world. These views have some value but they are not adequate in and of themselves.

*Biological immortality.*—Of course, we all want to live on in our children. However, it is obvious this is not a personal immortality.

*Social immortality.*—There is the influence of gifts, charities, books, good deeds, and living on in the memories of our friends. This has been called social immortality.

*Impersonal immortality.*—The Hindus talk of being absorbed like a drop of water into a higher self or Brahman or god. This is an impersonal concept.

*Subjective immortality.*—Modern process theologians often talk of being remembered in the mind of God. But in this study we are primarily concerned with personal immortality. This means living on as a unique individual beyond death.

### General Arguments for the Need of Life Beyond Death

Philosophers, religionists, and poets have suggested many general arguments for immortality, or life beyond death.

*The argument from history.*—All people seem to desire or want to believe in immortality. Like a homing pigeon, we say, man wants to make his way to God and fulfillment beyond death. Pyramids were built in order to assure immortality, or at least they thought, for the rulers of Egypt.

*The argument from justice and ethics.*—Immanuel Kant was perhaps the most weighty and significant philosopher of all time. Certainly his massive work has been a watershed for the development of modern thinking. Though skeptical about man's ability to prove immortality by reason alone, he offered a well-known argument for life after death.

Kant saw justice as an essential ingredient for a meaningful ethic. But he noticed at the same time that justice does not always prevail in this world. He observed what countless others have also observed: the righteous do suffer and the wicked often prosper in this life. His practical reason argued that since justice does not prevail here in this world there must be a place where it does prevail. For justice to exist ultimately there must be several factors accounted for. One, we must survive the grave. Two, there must be a judge. Three, there must be judgment.

Thus, for Kant, practical ethics require life after death and a judge whose description sounds very much like that of the God of Christianity. For Kant, life was intolerable without a solid basis for ethics. If death is ultimate, then no ethical mandate is really significant.

*The argument from incompleteness.*—Life, as we know it, seems so incomplete. Victor Hugo, at age seventy, wrote "Winter is on my head, but spring is in my heart. I have not said one thousandth part of what is in me."

*The argument from reason.*—For others, life is irrational if there is no hereafter. G. H. Palmer, as he looked at the body of his dead wife, killed in an automobile accident by a drunk driver, said, "This world is irrational if, because of a driver's careless turn, so fair a spirit is excluded forever from the universe."

### Widely-Held, Non-Christian Views of Last Things

If we look at humankind in a realistic and comprehensive way, it can be said that there are two basic non-Christian approaches or views of last things.

*The naturalistic approach (when you are dead, you are dead).*—This view sees life as only a physical process. Death is our absolute end. Our death means no more and no less than the death of other animals. It should be accepted without any illusion.

*The natural or innate immortality approach (make it under your own steam).*—This is the view of Plato, many Hindus, and the Spiritualists. Maybe one half of the people of the world hold this view.

Primitive view—Man believed from earliest times that in his body dwelt a "spirit" which at death departed and became a ghost. This approach was refined by Plato in the fourth century BC.

Plato and the Greeks—Plato faced the question of the life beyond in a deeply personal way when he visited his beloved teacher, Socrates, in his prison cell. As Socrates prepared himself for execution by the enforced drinking of hemlock (poison), he discussed the question of immortality with his students. The Socratic argument for life after death is recorded by Plato in his famous *Phaedo* dialogue. Plato stated that what is true and real is the world in us. Your soul is your divine and immortal essence. The body is its prison and is mortal. Your soul shares neither the birth nor the death of your body. Your soul preexisted. It is simple and does not die when your body decays. You can no more kill a soul than you can destroy a sunbeam with a sword. Death is not real. Your essential self, the soul, does not die at all. Holding this view, Socrates welcomed death as a friend. A similar view has been taken up by Christian Science in our time.

Classical Hinduism—The central idea of classical Hinduism is the natural immortality of the soul including preexistence and reincarnation. The soul budded off of Brahman and fell into a body. At death, the soul automatically lives on. It goes into a temporary heaven but is almost immediately reborn. The law of Karma, or automatic judgment, determines the next birth according to a person's conduct in a previous life. The ultimate goal of rebirths is reunion with Brahman or nirvana.

Despite some people's opinions, the Bible does not teach the preexistence of the human soul, natural or innate immortality, or the reincarnation of man.

Spiritualism—Closely related in many ways to the idealist views of Plato and the Hindus is Spiritualism. For the Spiritualist, man's soul is naturally immortal. You do not need God's power to live on beyond death. Most people automatically go to Summerland (the Spiritualist heaven) when they die. Through mediums and their helpers in Summerland, you can communicate with your loved ones. This is done in seances with the help of mediums.

The Bible is opposed to this view. This view has nothing about fellowship with God and no need of Christ. According to the Bible, man's greatest need is restored fellowship with God through Jesus Christ. The Bible forbids attempts to communicate with our loved ones through mediums (Deut. 18:10 *ff.*) or necromancers (talkers with the dead).

### Biblical and Christian View of Last Things

There are many aspects of last things which concern Christian doctrine, such as personal death and historical hope. The main thrust of the Christian hope, however, is that both personal life and historical life have a purpose and a conclusion. As we shall see, this Christian purpose and conclusion have implications for life before the end.

The New Testament and the majority of Christians through the centuries have not dwelt on the details of time, place, process, and personnel of last things. They have seen that the sense of expectancy which the New Testament teaches is not a matter of chronological timetables. But the sense of urgency should encourage a constant attitude of openness to the coming presence and judgment of God, in the light of which the Christian's attitude to the world is entirely changed.

And so, in Christian doctrine, it is best to stay with the central biblical truths, avoiding the temptation to say more than is required. The sovereignty of God does not rest comfortably with human pretensions to know too many details about the future. God indeed will keep his promises, but exactly how, when, and where lies within the freedom of God's will.

In the case of the Christian doctrine of last things, there is the necessary affirmation of an end point or second coming of Christ and a personal life beyond death. Christian doctrine speaks fundamentally about the nature and meaning of the end and is not preoccupied with the details of the particular method which God will use to bring us to the end.

*The resurrection of the dead.*—According to the Bible, we do not have a mortal part, the body, and a natural or innately immortal part, the soul, as separate entities. We are indivisible units—a body animated by a soul. Our hope for the life beyond is based on our relationship to God and the continuing power of God to recreate us beyond death with appropriate and identifiable resurrection bodies.

Because of our disobedience against God, we are separated from God. Death is related to this disobedience. Death is not beautiful. It is a dreaded enemy. For the early Israelites, it was a departure to the valley of shadows or Sheol—a place of gloom. According to the Bible, there is nothing in us unaided by God that can withstand the ravages of death.

But the good news of Christianity is that God's holiness and judgment are tempered by his mercy. He has conceived a love plan to restore our relationship to him and thus restore us to the possibility of new life here and now and eternal life hereafter.

Christ, himself sinless, endured death. Unlike the Greek philosopher, Socrates, who faced death with a smile, Jesus wept and trembled as he faced death. He cried out, "My God, my God, why hast thou forsaken me?" (Mark 15:34). Christ could conquer death only by actually dying. Paul called death the last enemy of God (1 Cor. 15:26).

Furthermore, if life is to issue out of so genuine a death as this, a new divine act of creation is necessary. Death must be conquered by the resurrection. Thus we see that Christ overcame the wages of sin which is death. He took our sins upon himself. "For our sake he made him to be sin who knew no sin, so that in him we might become the righteousness of God" (2 Cor. 5:21). He can free our inner selves now from the grip of sin and Satan. Later he can transform our outer body.

In Christ's resurrection, victory has been won. Paul stated that if Christ has not been raised from the dead, then those who have fallen asleep in Christ have perished (1 Cor. 15:18). But now Almighty God who raised Christ will give life to our mortal bodies (Rom. 8:11).

Our hope is not getting rid of our bodies but relating to God in Christ knowing that he can transform our bodies at death or give us a resurrection body. And in a preliminary way, we can know the power of the risen Christ even now in our inner selves. In spite of the fact that the Holy Spirit is already so powerfully at work, human beings must die. But beyond death is the resurrection body and the new heaven and the new earth. This is the Christian hope.

It cannot be emphasized too often that the main basis of man's hope, according to the biblical view, is not man's own natural or innate possession or power. Rather, it is God's power in Jesus Christ which is the assurance of God's plan to raise up to heaven those who have accepted Christ as the Messiah.

Christianity from the beginning was a historical religion and thus emphasized the historical life, death, and resurrection of Jesus Christ. All four of the Gospel writers emphasized the empty tomb. The apostle Paul gave us the earliest literary witness of the resurrection in 1 Corinthians 15. The historical value of this chapter is tremendous. Paul insisted that he passed on to the Corinthians the gospel he had received from the early preachers and witnesses who had seen Christ in his resurrection body. In fact, many of these witnesses were still living (1 Cor. 15:1,3-6).

It is not too much to say that the whole New Testament faith is closely related to the reality of the resurrection. If it had not been for the resurrection of Jesus, we would not have the New Testament nor the change to the Lord's day (first day) from the sabbath (seventh day). The early Christians were mostly Jews who had been nurtured in a Judaism which had emphasized the sanctity of the sabbath. Only the most revolutionary event could have enabled them to forsake the deeply established practice of worshiping on what we call Saturday and to worship on what we call Sunday or the Lord's Day (Rev. 1:10).

The Christian hope involves a resurrection body. The apostle Paul affirmed that there is no true life beyond without a body. But he also pointed out that in the economy of God there are various kinds of bodies—earthly and heavenly, perishable and imperishable, psychic and spiritual. Paul in 1 Corinthians did not accept the view taught by some Jewish writers (Baruch) which said that every particle of the physical body will be raised. Christians are not committed to a crude materialistic view of resurrection according to which the particles of the old body are somehow reassembled into the new.

On the other hand, there is a continuity between the body which is placed in the grave or cremated and the spiritual body, just as there is a continuity between a seed and the new plant. The creative power of God gives a new form to the life which sprouts from the seed. So God's power gives new form to our bodies which are sown as physical bodies but raised as spiritual bodies (1 Cor. 15:44).

Our resurrection body will be in some way like Christ's resurrection body because he is the firstfruits of those who have fallen asleep. The risen Lord was recognized and yet he was free from the limitations of space and time (John 20:27-29; Luke 24:13-35).

The resurrection will also involve a continuation of personal identity. The one whose body dies and who is transformed retains the same individual identity. Just as in nature it is this seed that will become that flower, so I will consciously experience the resurrection life. The word *body* is the nearest we come in the New Testament to our more abstract notions of identity and manner of existence (1 Cor. 15:37-38). The future life will be mine in a rich and meaningful way. The experience will not be reserved for some thinned-down entity such as a disembodied soul.

In fact, with the removal of earthly limitations, we will be more free to move in the direction of our deepest impulses and hence the true inner structure of our personality will be all the more evident. There will be no more possibility of camouflage. Perhaps we shall not only recognize one another but we shall know one another as God now knows us.

In other words, there is a change which is so great and complete that language runs out when we try to describe it. Paul could only remind us that, whereas life in the old body was marked by weakness, declining capacities, and the humiliation associated with failure and sin, the new mode of existence will be one of glory to which none of these limitations and defeats will apply. The significance of being "with Christ" and "in Christ" is surely better expressed in terms of life and growth rather than in terms of static perfection. The "mansions" (KJV) or "rooms" (RSV) of John 14:2 can be interpreted as temporary halting places for the redeemed personality on the journey onward and upward according to Westcott.

The center of the doctrine of the resurrection of the body is not just survival. That concern belongs to the very different idea of natural or innate immortality (a Greek and Hindu concept). The heart of resurrection is the transforming power of God, which changes a mode of existence marked by frailty and sin into a new form of life—one marked by power, glory, and the presence of the Holy Spirit.

Our Christian hope, then, is more than resuscitation of our corpse which has been buried in a cemetery or cremated. Our hope is that God will recreate us with an appropriate spiritual body which retains our unique identity.

*The second coming of Christ and the last judgment.*—In the first coming of Christ and the pouring out of the Holy Spirit, the kingdom is already present in one sense. In the Gospel of John we have this emphasis upon the present availability of the resources of the kingdom for the Christians. John 3:36 says that he who believes has eternal life. Some scholars of our time have gone so far as to talk about "realized eschatology." This view affirms that practically everything Christ has for us is given to us in his first coming and in the pouring out of the Holy Spirit.

As we have seen in the chapter "The Guiding Key," the best contemporary Christian scholarship, however, emphasizes that the second coming of Christ is very important if a person is to properly understand the New Testament. The fullness of the kingdom is yet to come. One scholar has said that the first coming only inaugurated or initiated the kingdom. Satan's hold has been undermined but by no means completely destroyed. The Son of man must appear again, this time in glory and triumph. The Christian community lived in the confidence that what had been inaugurated and initiated would be carried to completion. Fulfillment of the promises has been guaranteed but it has not yet been fully achieved.

The resurrection has taken place, and the Holy Spirit has come as a down payment (see Eph. 1:14). Christ reigns invisibly now through the eyes of faith, but he will reign visibly at that great day.

Our final resurrection body and the last judgment will be related to the second coming of Christ. Paul said, "So also in Christ shall all be made alive" (1 Cor. 15:22). In rich dramatic language, the Bible tells of Christ's coming in power and glory. Christian saints who have died will be raised to meet Christ. Christians living will be transformed to meet him (1 Thess. 4:16-17).

Appropriate resurrection bodies will be given to us at the last judgment and the basic orientation and quality of our life will be unveiled.

The root meaning for the *judgment* is separation or division (2 Cor. 5:10). The Judge on the last day is not to be thought of as a courtroom judge who decides the destiny of the accused. Our ultimate destiny was decided when we accepted or rejected Christ. Rather, the Judge is like the judge of an art exhibit or an oratorical contest who discriminates between a good performance and a poor one. The decision of your destiny has already taken place before the final judgment.

The final judgment makes clear those who have responded inwardly and truly. The New Testament stresses that the practical basis for the final discrimination is a quality of life as expressed in your deeds. There is no conflict between this and justification by faith through grace. There is no contradiction in saying that a person is saved by grace and yet judged by works. Grace is a creative power by which the new life in the Spirit is generated. Works are the fruit of the new life. The gospel always presents a person's deeds as an indication of the total quality of a person's life. For example, unless the faith which appropriates God's forgiveness manifests itself as a forgiving disposition toward other people, it is not a true faith.

But even among believers on the judgment day, there are differences. A relevant passage is found in 1 Corinthians 3:11-15. For the Christian who has sought his own glory and demonstrated vain pretensions unlike the mind of Christ, his personality structure is built of wood, hay, and stubble which the fire of judgment will destroy. The believer is not allowed to enter his final destiny with a false estimate of himself. Although his shoddy or inferior works are thus made manifest, the forgiveness of sins in Christ still holds; and he is saved. Thus the end is a life everlasting with true humility and with a consciousness of his need for further growth in Christ.

Some theologians who accept the revealed truth that Jesus Christ died for the sins of the whole world maintain that this means that everyone will be saved in the end. It is reasoned that, since the fall has affected us all and since God's grace in Jesus is for everyone, it is only logical that everyone will be saved. *The idea may seem logical, but it is not biblical.* It overlooks the essential biblical conditions for salvation—repentance and faith.

The New Testament description of God's judgment on sin makes it clear that each person is accountable to God for his use of freedom. Sin will not go unpunished. Though God's love has provided a way of forgiveness for every sinner, God's justice makes everyone accountable for his or her own choice. God does not force his will on people, rather he invites them to respond. Each person has an option. This fact calls persons to repentance and faith. There is hell and judgment. We know absolutely nothing of the proportion of the saved to the lost but this we do know, that none will be lost unless they refuse the grace of God revealed in the cosmic and historical Christ.

*Hell.*—Every sincere Christian shudders at the thought of hell and anyone rejecting Christ. But we must not set up our own standards of God's love and justice. The Bible does indicate that those who have not heard of the historic Christ do have a revelation of God and the cosmic Christ in conscience and nature. But Paul in Romans 1 stated that they have not even accepted this light and followed it. They too have rejected Christ. Even for those people, hell can be described as a person's choice to be excluded from the presence of God (Rom. 1:20-32; Col. 1:15-16).

It is Christ who said there is a "hell where . . . the fire is not quenched" (Mark 9:47-48). Christ will have to say to those at his left hand, "Depart from me, you cursed, into the eternal fire prepared for the devil and his angels" (Matt. 25:41).

Judgment and hell are a dark reality, but they do not stand at the center of Jesus' teaching about human destiny. "For God sent the Son into the world, not to condemn the world, but that the world might be saved through him" (John 3:17). He holds out to all people the opportunity to accept from him the glorious privilege of eternal life.

*Heaven.*—The Christian hope involves the new heaven and the new earth. There is a minimum of speculation about the new heaven and the new earth in the New Testament. The central emphasis is on the fact that Christ is Lord. A major emphasis is upon a transformed earth. The matter of geography is not as central as the emphasis on worship and righteousness. Heaven will surely involve relief, reward, realization, appreciation, and endless growth.

There are enough hints in the Bible to understand that heaven is not just dull continuance. It will surely involve some memory. There will be recognition. In fact, we will know each other more thoroughly than now (1 Cor. 13:12). There will be no possibility of camouflage. There will surely be a new kind of alternation between work and rest. It is a time of life and growth.

The biblical writers stretched language to its limits to describe the beauty and bliss of that perfect state. But every image and metaphor points even beyond this to the beauty of him who is its source. Heaven is not to be thought of as the static perfection of the frozen shot at the end of a film. God is the living God, whose presence holds forth the promise of the ever new. So the declining capacities and failing opportunities of earthly life are replaced by their opposite: a growing period of glory and an element of surprise.

### The Relation of Last Things to this Life

The usual criticism of a strong emphasis upon hope and the life hereafter is that it causes people to become too other-worldly. Communists contend that Christianity is a religion of "pie in the sky by and by." Actually the biblical hope properly understood is not other-worldly. It is related to life here and now. It is really a fulfillment of the gains, experiences, and labors of this age. For example, the resurrection of the body shows a continuity between personal life in this age and the person in community life in the age to come. Therefore, the biblical world view properly understood, does not encourage withdrawal from life or a negative view of history.

Even nature is to share in the renewed creation. This means that nature is significant. Such a view of nature constitutes the proper background for science. This is not the view of certain forms of Hinduism which teach that nature is semiillusory or *maya* or less than significant.

In fact, the biblical view of hope has many helpful emphases. It holds out the ideal of the new heaven and the new earth which has no place for an improper individualism or cultural and racial discrimination. The biblical view of hope also affirms the reality and meaning of historical time without falling into the delusion of Communism which is that time and history can fulfill themselves.

G. Beasley-Murray points out that biblical hope, including the second coming of Christ, undergirds an intense present. This hope gives incentive to action. It gives Christians a prophetic freedom which enables them to be more firm and decisive in regard to ethical matters. It gives Christians a personal dynamic. This expectant attitude also gives a solid sense of responsibility. The Coming One is the Lord and Judge to whom we must be prepared to give an account of our stewardship of time and influence and talents. The apostle Paul said that in light of our hope in

Christ we are to be steadfast, unmovable, always abounding in the work of the Lord (1 Cor. 15:58).

## Conclusion

As evangelical Christians we cannot embrace the naturalist, Greek, Hindu, and Spiritualist beliefs. We can, however, offer to the world from our own Christian resources a dynamic and superior alternative. We believe that only the Word of the living God has the resources to fill the vacuum in our national and personal lives. There is hope for us now and hereafter in Christ. It is the responsibility and privilege of each Christian to incarnate this hope in our lives and share its joy and significance with others.

### Notes

1. Robin Keeley, ed., *Eerdmans' Handbook to Christian Belief* (Grand Rapids, MI: Wm. B. Eerdmans, 1982), pp. 382-384.

2. Ibid., pp. 397-399.

3. William W. Wells, *Welcome to the Family: An Introduction to Evangelical Christianity* (Downers Grove, IL: InterVarsity Press, 1979), pp. 172-173.

4. W. T. Conner, *Christian Doctrine* (Nashville: Broadman Press, 1937), p. 264.

5. Keeley, pp. 374-375.

### Bibliography

Conner, W.T. *Christian Doctrine.* Nashville: Broadman Press, 1937.

Cullman, Oscar. *Immortality of the Soul; or Resurrection from the Dead?* New York: Macmillan, 1958.

Keeley, Robin, ed. *Eerdmans' Handbook to Christian Belief.* Grand Rapids, MI: Wm. B. Eerdmans, 1982.

Newport, John P. "The Theology and Experience of Salvation." *The Greek Orthodox Theological Review,* Vol. XXII, No. 4 (Winter 1977): 393-404.

Wells, William W. *Welcome to the Family: An Introduction to Evangelical Christianity.* Downers Grove, IL: InterVarsity Press, 1979.

# 9

# The Urgency of the Persuasive Presentation and Sharing of Christian Doctrine

The United States and many other countries of the world have almost made a fetish or idol of reason and education. Most people either want a college education or want their children or grandchildren to have one. It follows for some people that, since reason and secular education are so powerful, they can provide a completely adequate basis for life apart from any special revelation from God.

Since God created man with reason, we should not see reason as evil. However, since man's fall, reason has its limits and distortions, especially in the area of God-man and person-person relationships.

A minister tells of his visit to a prison which had an extensive educational program for the prisoners. One criminal was overheard telling another: "I am taking a course in higher accounting. You should enroll in the class. If you don't, when we get out you will just continue to be an ordinary thief while I will be a high-up embezzler." This incident points out that reason—as important as it is—can be used for harmful purposes.

On the other hand, Christians are told by Peter that we should use our reason and always be prepared to make a defense to anyone who calls us to account for the hope that is in us (1 Pet. 3:15). The word "defense" used by Peter is the Greek word *apologia,* which means a defense of the Christian faith. Peter made a direct appeal for Christians to engage in apologetics. This does not mean an apology in the usual sense of the word. Apologetics is an attempt to show the truth of the Christian faith in a persuasive way.

Of course, there are some Christians who do not want to use reason because they see reason as complicated and they think that Christianity should be simple. Furthermore, they see reason as intellectual and for them Christianity should be "spiritual." They even argue that the apostle

Paul was opposed to reason when he wrote in 1 Corinthians 1:21 that "since, in the wisdom of God, the world did not know God through wisdom, it pleased God through the folly of what we preach to save those who believe." But we must remember that Paul was in no way suggesting that the gospel is actually foolish or irrational. He meant only that it is seen as foolish or folly in the eyes of people who do not believe. Paul went on to say that it is the non-Christian thinking or philosophy which is in truth foolish. In contrast, the Christian message is the only true wisdom (vv. 18-25).

Christians affirm the limitations of natural or unregenerate wisdom, especially in the area of God-man relations. But Christians should be prepared to use reason, renewed by Christ, to show the validity and power of the Christian answer to man's basic questions. We should seek to show that the Christian faith answers the universal problems and questions of human life more adequately than any other world view or doctrine.

## Basic Approaches to Faith and Reason

In order to see more clearly the proper approach to the relation between faith and reason, note three approaches which have been used in Western culture.

### Reason First—Then Faith

Thomas Aquinas, who lived in the thirteenth century, was one of the greatest Christian thinkers in the Middle Ages. His famous book *The Sum of Theology Against the Gentiles* was, among other things, a lengthy manual for Christian missionaries to help them to persuade non-Christians, especially Muslims, to become Christians. According to Aquinas, man's mind is capable of discovering most truth by the exercise of reason alone, independent of special revelation from God.

This view of the relation between faith and reason, developed by Thomas Aquinas, has been called the two-story approach. Human reason is the ground floor of the human knowledge of God. Through natural reasoning you can prove God's existence and establish many of God's qualities. Through reason you can learn of human freedom and establish the immortality of the human soul. For Aquinas, human reason was not seriously marred in the fall of man.

However, according to the view of Aquinas, reason can only erect the ground floor. Divine revelation must build the second story. It is only through special or divine revelation that we learn of Christ's incarnation, his redemptive death, and his resurrection. Revelation thus enriches and completes reason.

The position of Aquinas has become the dominant view of the Roman Catholic Church. But there are also a number of orthodox Protestant thinkers who are quite close to the ideas of Thomas Aquinas in their views. For example, B. B. Warfield, the famous Princeton orthodox theologian, believed that although the Holy Spirit is necessary to produce "saving" faith, reason can produce the grounds for such faith. Christianity, Warfield believed, has been placed in the world to reason its way to a position of influence.

### Faith (Revelation) Is Primary and Reason Has Only Limited Value

In some cases this view stakes itself directly and without critical examination on what is believed. No further evidence or argument is needed. For example, some Christians accept Christian beliefs without examination since they are personally convinced of their truth no matter what. These Christians do not think it necessary to weigh their view against anyone else's nor do they examine the self-consistency and range of application of their view. This type of "faith-only" approach belittles the use of reason.

*Luther and reason.*—Martin Luther (1483-1546), an Augustinian monk, started his religious quest with a question, How do I find a gracious God? Since he saw the perfect God and fallen human nature as enemies, he concluded that we are reconciled to God only through God's gracious coming in Jesus Christ. We can know God only as he reveals himself to us in his Word and promises.

Because of his belief in the priority of the revelation to fallen man in Jesus Christ, Luther often sounded as if he distrusted reason. In truth, Luther believed that reason was helpful to the Christian. What Luther opposed was not reason but the attempt of fallen man to use reason in making a ladder to climb to heaven in man's own wisdom and power.

*Pascal and reason.*—Blaise Pascal (1623-1662), the French scientist and Christian writer, sketched out his approach to reason in a book called *Pensees.* Pascal, influenced by Augustine, believed that the certainties of faith are attained only through the heart that loves. Pascal did not despise reason, but he saw man in a moral and spiritual dilemma where reason by itself is not enough. When Christ comes to us, he is beyond our ability to explain in rational categories. And yet Christ invites us to follow him and then we shall know the truth of his claims. It is the heart (the whole being) which experiences and knows God and not just the reason. Submission to God does not necessarily go against reason, but beyond it.

Both Luther and Pascal are sometimes seen to set revelation and reason sharply against each other. They do guard the truth that we know God only as he chooses to reveal himself. This approach is in contrast to the teaching of some systems of philosophy and world religions which say that man is divine and can know God by his own reasoning. Only God can reveal God. The saving or redemptive knowledge of God is a gift from God himself and is not at our disposal.

*Augustine and Anselm and reason.*—Both Augustine (354-430) and Anselm (1033-1109) developed the idea of believing reason. They used the phrase "Believe in order to understand." They also spoke of their approach as "Faith Seeking Understanding." The idea of faith, or the commitment of the whole person to the self-revelation of God as having the primary place, does not in the least play down reason and evidence but rather shows their proper and essential place.

Anselm affirmed that reason, like faith, is a gift of God. If faith convinces a person of the truth of God's self-revelation in Jesus Christ, then surely reason will be able to help a person understand and share this truth.

*Barth and reason.*—Karl Barth, the famous Swiss theologian, is oftentimes misunderstood in the area of the relation of faith and reason. Barth does say that we cannot first establish Christianity as true in terms of some philosophical or rational test and then transfer that conviction to the truths of the gospel. Oranges cannot verify apples. Unaided reason cannot prove the gospel.

The special revelation of God in Jesus Christ by grace does have a content of truth in it which in turn speaks to the human reason. Barth believes that in Anselm's program we can use reason safely and properly in a Christian way. Barth would say with Anselm, "I believe, Lord help me to understand what my heart has already believed."

One must have a Christianized reason. Reason is Christianized by the grace of God, the Holy Spirit, and the saving gospel of Jesus Christ. Then that Christianized reason can do its utmost to explore and present to others the depths of Christian theology. According to Barth, this "Christianization of reason" is precisely Anselm's achievement and the point of the central failure of Thomas Aquinas and those who follow his approach. Their idea is that reason comes first and then faith. In contrast, Anselm and Barth would say "We can follow our reason if it is Christianized, with no fear that it will ever turn on us."

## Context in the Persuasive Presentation of Christian Doctrine

A missionary told of an experience he had while teaching methods of Christian witness in Africa. He had spent several hours in presenting arguments for the existence of God. After one of the classes, he was approached by a student. After some hemming and hawing, the student finally had the courage to say, "Nobody here really needs to know about these arguments for the existence of God. Very few people here have any doubt that God exists. In fact, they believe in many gods. Our question is, *which* god should we obey." This teacher was getting a good lesson in the importance of understanding the context and background of the people to whom we are talking about Christian doctrine.

I had a similar experience when I was trying to prove that Jesus Christ was divine to a Hindu professor. Before I could give my arguments for the divinity of Jesus, the Hindu professor said, "I believe that Jesus Christ is the divine Son of God." In my ignorance of Hindu doctrine, I at first thought that we were in agreement. But I came to find out that this professor believed that there were many other divine sons of God, including several Hindu incarnations of God. For this Hindu professor, Jesus Christ was only one of many divine revealers of God or saviors.

Every situation, every culture, indeed every person has certain needs which the gospel is meant to satisfy. The genius of Christianity is that it is relevant to all human need. It is up to us to get close enough to people to know where these needs exist, to hear the questions that they may not even be able to clearly explain and to apply the gospel just where it is needed.

## The Importance of the Practical Approach

In our persuasive presentation of Christian doctrine, it is important to use the practical approach. There are six methods which can be used in this approach.

## The Basic Questions Method

This method seeks to establish the truthfulness of Christianity by asking certain basic questions which must be answered by any world view or religion which seeks to command the allegiance of men.

*Is it more reasonable to believe that the universe was created by a personal God or that it came into being by itself, by chance?*

*Is there convincing evidence for the historical events recorded in the Bible which have become the basis for Christian beliefs about God and about Jesus?*—For instance, what sort of historical evidence is there for the Exodus of the Israelites from Egypt or the resurrection of Jesus? Have we a firm enough basis to believe that these are real, historical events?

## The Constructive Answers to Criticism Method

A second practical method is to give constructive answers to criticisms. In the early days of Christianity, the Christian apologists replied to specific hostile attacks on the Christian faith. Twentieth-century Christians must continue to answer attacks on the Christian faith. The apostle Paul in Philippians 1:16 stated that Christians are to throw themselves vigorously into the defense of the gospel.

A significant group of criticisms of Christianity in our time is related to the development of psychology. We will look at four criticisms and a brief Christian answer to each. One criticism is that Christian experience can be explained by naturalistic and psychological factors in our past experience. The Christian answers by showing that the moral direction of life is reversed in Christian conversion.

Another criticism is that Christian conversion is a form of father projection. The Christian answers that God uses the relationship with our male parent as a normal way to understand God as our Father.

A third psychological criticism suggests that Christianity is suppressed sexuality. The Christian shows that there is no necessary correlation between marriage or a sexual state and Christian conversion.

A fourth criticism states that Christian experience is a form of psychological escapism from the difficulties and demands of life. The Christian points out that authentic Christianity calls for the Christian to live a life of sacrifice, stewardship, and discipline.

Of course, Christian scholars have been able to provide far more detailed and constructive answers to these criticisms than the brief statements made here.

## The Removal of Misunderstandings and Barriers Method

It is important to remove the occasions of stumbling over Christianity caused by misunderstanding. In some cases, this misunderstanding prevents the non-Christian from seeing the Christian faith as it really is. Christianized reason can help remove these barriers to faith.

## The Avoidance of Blind Belief Method

If reason is not used in certain cases, there is little to prevent people from accepting distorted forms of Christianity or non-Christian faiths. As one Christian scholar has said, "If Christian faith is nothing but a blind leap into the dark then I might as well leap to Muhammed, or to Buddha, or to Mary Baker Glover Patterson Eddy and become a Christian Scientist."

One thing that would save us from this approach would be what Martin Luther called the negative function of reason. Reason can tell us where revelation has not taken place. Not all self-proclaimed revelations can be true, for many religious writings which are self-described as "revelations" contradict one another. In other cases, they lead to harmful actions and attitudes. In certain cases, the "revelations" can be shown to be based on fraud or plagiarism.

## The Restatement of the Biblical World-View Method

Since we can purchase a copy of the Bible in a variety store for very little money, we sometimes forget that the future of Western culture may turn on what people do with the material which lies between the covers of the Bible.

Christian doctrine involves teachings that are vital for every area of life and thought. These teachings need to be developed and described so non-Christians can see the richness and depth of the Christian world view. We must point out the negative influence of non-Christian teachings and show the superiority of the Christian ones. Christian apologetics seeks to identify and systematically make clear these Christian distinctives in relation to the world of ideas.

## The Verification or Testing Method

We can measure alternative world views or doctrinal systems by several yardsticks. Sometimes these tests are expressed in a popular manner. For example, alternative world views can be measured by the following three tests: how well do they fit with the world as we experience it? What sort of effect do they have on the people who adopt them? How valid a purpose do they offer for our lives?

But these tests can be described in a more formal way.

*The first test is that of consistency.*—Do the elements of Christianity which constitute it as a world view hang together? Does Christianity make sense? Is it a consistent system in which all parts fit together? Does it have structure and wholeness?

Within the academic evangelical community, Gordon Clark of Butler University has been one of the most influential apologists of the modern era. Clark's lifelong task has been to show that non-Christian viewpoints are inconsistent and that Christianity is most consistent. His *Christian View of Men and Things* is the classic statement of his view.

*The second test is that of comprehensiveness.*—This test affirms that an adequate world view should be able to explain and make sense of all kinds of human experience and authenticated scientific data.

A world view must explain love and hate, as well as creativity and destruction. It must explain humanity's longing for truth and personal fulfillment, as well as the inability of sheer physical pleasure or money to satisfy completely. There is also an explanation needed for humanity's refusal to operate in a completely nonmoral fashion. In other words, this test evaluates world views in relation to the completeness with which they integrate things into a unified and meaning-giving whole.

*The third test is that of personal and cultural satisfaction and relevance.*—It should be obvious that an adequate world view should be personally satisfactory and fulfilling. It must meet our sense of personal need.

This test also asks if our world view has community and cultural relevance. If Christianity is what we claim for it, we should see evidence for its truth both in our own lives and in the life of the Christian community and in history. Christianity claims that there is such evidence.

First, personal Christian experience is universally claimed to be based on the historical and exalted Christ. That all Christian testimony agrees on this point provides basic experiential evidence for the existence and reality of such a figure. One would have to deny the reality of these experiences with their consistent testimony in order to cast doubt on the reality of Christ.

Similarity of Christian testimony increases its weight as evidence. Christian experience always centers around personal fellowship with the Savior, claimed by Christians to be the Son of God. In court, witnesses gain credence to the degree that their testimony agrees. Thus the believability of Christian testimony becomes stronger because of this agreement.

There are those who say that this experience of Christ is a delusion. Christians may honestly feel that they are experiencing what in fact cannot be experienced. But clinical evidence suggests that behavior consistently based on a delusion has a destructive effect on the personality. Christianity, however, more often than not, has a positive moral and spiritual effect on the believer. Christians claim that Christ helps make men and women whole, and there is evidence to support this claim.[1]

Francis Schaeffer pioneered an approach which has been called cultural apologetics. In his book *The God Who Is There,* he argues that by examining modern cultures we can see that loss of faith in God breaks down cultural values and leads to dehumanization and loss of satisfaction.

Schaeffer's method is to examine the view of a culture as it is revealed in its art and literature. In the West, tracing the decline of faith in God, one can show how unbelief leads to human disorientation and confusion. This is seen on every hand in modern art and literature. And yet, since we are created for God and cannot live without him, we refuse to believe life is meaningless. This means that we insist on committing ourselves to causes, falling in love, and creating grand symbols of our quests in art and literature. In this attempt to create meaning, Schaeffer claims, we are being inconsistent. We are living off of Christian values, even as we deny their source. To approach such people, we must point out their inconsistency. Schaeffer calls this "taking the roof off " people and showing them where they really live. When they see that, apart from God, none of their pursuits has any meaning, we can present the Christian gospel to them and tell them that it alone can give them satisfaction and meaning.[2]

In mission fields, especially in Third-World countries, the proof of

Christianity oftentimes comes in terms of a power encounter with other religious systems. According to the Bible, humanity exists in a conflict of powers, in the struggle of Satan against God. People are forced to act and decide. They must take sides in this great struggle, and the Spirit of the biblical God must be shown to be greater and more powerful than rival spirits and gods. This is an actual power confrontation taking place in people's experience, not merely a theoretical conflict which must be understood. When Christianity arrived in the Solomon Islands, conversions resulted from the confrontation of the power of God with primitive gods.

If the Christian faith is rooted in history, we should be able to find public evidences of its power. The Christian claims that such support is not lacking. Within secular history, God's kingdom activity is clearly visible to those with eyes to see it. The primary evidence exists in the worldwide spread and vitality of the Christian movement.

There are many evidences of the power of Christianity. For example, no religion has had the effect of Christianity on human speech and language. Wherever Christianity has gone, it has concerned itself with language and translation. Believing in the importance of the revealed Word of God, Christians have worked to make it widely available.

Christianity has also fostered education wherever its missionaries have gone. Christians have always been concerned to teach their converts to read and write.

Christian missionaries have provided medicine and hospitals throughout the world. In many cases, Christianity has championed women's rights. William Carey fought for years against the Hindu practice of burning widows on their husbands' funeral pyres and finally succeeded in obtaining a decree against it. Missionaries fought also to abolish the Chinese practice of footbinding. All these reforms grew out of the Christian view that all people are God's creation, have value, and stand equally before him. Of course, Christians have not always lived up to the principles of the Christian faith.

The obvious contributions of Christianity are only the tip of the iceberg. The real miracles and changes and satisfactions are less visible but more widespread. These include the work of forgiveness and renewal that God does in hearts, families, and communities in countless unknown places and unremembered times.[3]

Thus we can say that there is a definite Christian world view which has a character, consistency, and unity of its own. It stands in sharp contrast with counter theories and speculations. Furthermore, this world view has the stamp of reason and reality upon it and can amply justify itself at the bar of both history and experience.

## The Importance of the Basic Biblical Concepts Approach

This approach can be compared to an interesting building project in a large city which attracts its sidewalk superintendents. When the Christian community carefully and attractively constructs its basic system of doctrine, it should attract interested onlookers. An important way to persuasively present and share Christian doctrine is not a defensive mind-set which sits back and waits for attacks. Rather, there should be a positive expression of what we believe to be true about God, the person, and the world.

Although we seek to answer representative objections to Christianity, it is even more important to present to the world a basic framework of doctrine in terms of which objections can be met. The challenges that face Christianity change rapidly and depend on shifting circumstances. Therefore, it is impossible to foresee specific answers which we might one day be called upon to give. In fact, one purpose of this introductory volume on Christian doctrine is to give a generalized, suggestive, and integrative overview of the Christian world view.

Karl Barth once described a well-constructed Christian doctrinal system as a great cathedral. It is a thing of beauty, and, as we perceive the whole Christian doctrinal system, we have a satisfying experience of the beautiful. If Christian theology is like a cathedral, it then has a beauty and attractiveness of its own. The Word of God shines in its beauty and glory. In other words, Christian doctrine carries its divine credentials and appealing power within itself. The final apologetics of the Christian faith is the power of the Christian system of doctrine to glow, to radiate, and to be luminous in its own light.[4]

## The Importance of the Approach of Being

Perhaps the most needed approach in our time is not just in terms of thinking but in terms of "being." For example, *agape* love's superiority to secular motivation and an impersonal Eastern compassion must be demonstrated in terms of unselfish service. Christian people must live out and make use of Christian resources. Christian laypersons must not forget that "being" is one of our important avenues of sharing and witness in the secular world. The early Christians not only outthought but also outlived and outdied the pagans. We must set our Christian house in order in terms of "being" every day.

For the Christian, a related way to communicate "being" is to be sure that the loving presence of God is visible in communities (churches) that come together in his name. Openness, forgiveness, and hospitality should characterize such fellowships. Christians should join God's renewal program in the world. We must not only have opinions but also make plans. If it is true that Christianity is a project in history by which God is doing something about the world's fallen condition, then it is also true that we can work with him toward this end.

We must remember Peter's promise at Pentecost that by the Spirit would come power to do great things for God (Acts 2:17). For as Christ has given us "power to become children of God" (John 1:12), so he can make God's kingdom visible not "in talk but in power" (1 Cor. 4:20). Clearly if this power is not seen in our lives and in our communities (churches) it is a reproach to our faith.

The rational presentation of doctrine is important to our faith, but Christianity is far more than a system of thought. The spiritual renewal that we yearn for is not just one of ideas but of events, of happenings, and of a mighty spiritual movement reaching down to the masses of people.

As important as is Christian doctrine and the understanding of a biblical doctrinal system, to accept the Christian world view only as an intellectual system is not to accept it fully. There is a deeply personal dimension involved in living within this biblical world view. It involves acknowledging our own individual dependence on God as his creatures, our own individual rebellion against God, and our own individual dependence on God for restoration to fellowship with him. And it means accepting Jesus Christ as both our Liberator from bondage and the Lord of our future.

To be a Christian who has embraced the biblical world view is to be personally committed to the personal and infinite Creator God as he is revealed in Jesus Christ. And we believe that this commitment leads to the fulfilled life as God intended for us to live.

In the final analysis, we cannot intellectually argue people into accepting the Christian world view. But we are charged with the responsibility for the proclamation and presentation of the biblical world view in every way possible, including an intellectual presentation.[5]

In conclusion, we now realize, as G. K. Chesterton once said, "If you do not believe in God, you will not believe in nothing. Rather you will believe anything." This means that all people have some type of world view or doctrine. The Christian conviction is that the Christian world view is the only God-ordained, fulfilling, and saving view for persons who are made in God's image. The underlying purpose, therefore, of the study of Christian doctrine is not only to undergird personal faith and understanding but also to seek to be used of God to persuasively present and share the Christian faith with all people.

### Notes

1. William Dyrness, *Christian Apologetics in a World Community* (Downers Grove, IL: InterVarsity Press, 1983), pp. 67-68.

2. Ibid., p. 68.

3. Ibid., pp. 76-81.

4. Bernard Ramm, *After Fundamentalism: The Future of Evangelical Theology* (San Francisco: Harper & Row, 1983), p. 64.

5. James W. Sire, *The Universe Next Door* (Downers Grove, IL: InterVarsity Press, 1976), p. 214.

### Bibliography

Bush, L. Russ, ed. *Classical Readings in Christian Apologetics, A.D. 100-1800.* Grand Rapids, MI: The Zondervan Corporation, 1983.

Dyrness, William. *Christian Apologetics in a World Community.* Downers Grove, IL: InterVarsity Press, 1983.

Newport, John P. *Christ and the New Consciousness.* Nashville: Broadman Press, 1978.
_____. *Christianity and Contemporary Art Forms.* Waco: Word, Inc., 1971.

Ramm, Bernard. *After Fundamentalism: The Future of Evangelical Theology.* San Francisco: Harper & Row, 1983.

Sire, James W. *The Universe Next Door.* Downers Grove, IL: InterVarsity Press, 1976.